A Woman's Guide to Better Golf

Judy Rankin

with Peter McCleery

CONTEMPORARY BOOKS

A TRIBUNE COMPANY

Library of Congress Cataloging-in-Publication Data

Rankin, Judy.
    A woman's guide to better golf / Judy Rankin with Peter
McCleery.
        p.   cm.
    Includes index.
    ISBN 0-8092-3406-8 (cloth)
    ISBN 0-8092-3126-3 (paper)
    1. Golf for women.   I. McCleery, Peter.   II. Title.
GV966.R36   1995
796.352'024042—dc20   95-25500
                                   CIP

Cover design by Monica Baziuk
Front cover photograph by Jim Moriarty
Author photograph on back cover by Jeff Hornback
Interior design by Frank Loose Design

Principal instructional photography by Jim Moriarty. Also
supplying photos: Jeff Hornback, Paul Lester, *Golf Digest*, and
the Mercantile Library, St. Louis, Missouri. Illustrations by Ken
Lewis. Special thanks to IBIS Golf and Country Club in West
Palm Beach, Florida, and Indigo Lakes Golf Club in Daytona
Beach, Florida, the locations for the instructional photos.

Published by Contemporary Books
An imprint of NTC/Contemporary Publishing Company
Two Prudential Plaza, Chicago, Illinois 60601-6790
Manufactured in the United States of America
International Standard Book Number: 0-8092-3406-8 (cloth)
                                          0-8092-3126-3 (paper)
10   9   8   7   6   5   4   3   2   1

This book is dedicated to the men in my life who always encouraged me and never quit.

—J.R.

CONTENTS

Foreword by Paul Azinger   *vii*

Preface   *ix*

Introduction   *xi*

1 *Overcoming the Intimidation Factor*   *1*

2 *Beginning for Beginners: The 7-Iron, 30-Day Test*   *5*

3 *The Grip: Getting Your Hands on the Club Correctly*   *11*

4 *Getting Ready: Posture, Address, and Alignment*   *23*

5 *The Full Swing: Loading Up and Letting Go*   *37*

6 *Putting: The Stroke, the Speed, and the Read*   *69*

7 *The Short Game: Chipping and Pitching*   *93*

8 *Bunker Play: You Don't Need Dynamite to Escape the Sand*   *109*

9 *Specialized Shots—Trouble and Otherwise*   *127*

10 *Exercise: Warming Up and Stretching Out*   *139*

11 *Equipment: It Can Help, If You Get the Proper Fit*   *147*

12 *The LPGA Tour: Competition and Opportunity*   *159*

13 *Television: What I've Learned, and What You Can Learn from It*   *167*

14 *The Mental Side: Smart Strategy and Staying Positive*   *173*

15 *Giving and Taking Lessons: Building Rapport and Creating Independence*   *181*

16 *Keeping It Fun*   *187*

The Rankin File   *189*

Index   *191*

FOREWORD

by Paul Azinger

When I was growing up in Sarasota, Florida, my parents were members of Bent Tree Golf and Country Club. I'll never forget when the LPGA Tour came to town in 1977. The pro there was saying that none of these women would break 70 that week. I went out to watch the first day and saw Judy Rankin shoot 63. She went on to win the tournament—and immediately became one of my golfing idols.

I can still recall seeing her out on the sixth hole. She was just lighting up the place. She had kind of skinny arms, and that made her left-hand grip stand out all the more. It was turned far more to the right, with all the knuckles of the left hand showing in a "strong" position, than almost anyone I'd ever seen. Judy was the first player who really showed you could play with a grip like that. At the time, to tell you the truth, I didn't even know what a "strong" grip was. But I was naturally inclined to hold the club in the same way, and in Judy I found a kindred spirit. Seeing her and how she hit the ball really convinced me that my grip was OK. After watching her that week, I knew that I didn't have to change my grip. And I haven't.

That "strong" grip has now become much more prevalent on the tour. Some of the game's top players—from Fred Couples to Laura Davies—are using the same grip that Judy and I have used all our lives. It's just more acceptable now. If you've got the strongest player on the LPGA Tour using it, you know you don't have to be a weaker player to use a strong grip anymore. But I agree with Judy: This grip makes a lot of sense for many players, and especially women who are trying to generate more distance and power.

I didn't actually meet Judy until many years later when she was working for ABC Sports and I was playing in the 1988 U.S. Open in Brookline, Massachusetts. She came over to cover my group. I was so pleased to see her, and I told her how much I admired her. I used to be self-conscious when one of the other on-course commentators followed me. I got some criticism about my grip being "too strong," as I'm sure Judy did. I used to wonder what they were thinking or saying about me. But when Judy followed me, I didn't have to worry about that. I played better. She gave me confidence. She told me I had vindicated her and given her grip new credibility! We've since formed a mutual admiration society of sorts, and I always look forward to seeing her—for one thing, it means I must be playing well because I'm getting some airtime!

Judy does a great job whether she's on the course or up in the booth. She's an incredible lady, first class all the way, and she never intrudes or gets in the way of the players. She gives you the information you need, gets in and out, and moves on. She has credibility with us because she's been there. I believe the commentators who have been through the heat of battle themselves can offer the most insight into what's happening on the golf course, and Judy's been there many times. She had such a great career. She taught me a lot. And she'll teach you a lot in this book.

PREFACE

I first got to know Judy Rankin about 10 years ago when she was doing the U.S. Women's Open at Baltusrol. She stood out among the crowd even then. I go in with a huge bias—that most of the people broadcasting golf on television aren't very good. They either don't offer much insight or don't know how to communicate clearly—sometimes both—or talk too much, the worst crime of all. Judy was guilty on none of these counts. In fact, I believe what distinguishes her is her unobtrusive, no-nonsense delivery— she basically just gives you the facts with little embellishment, never trying to insert herself as part of the story. At the same time, she has a knack for telling you something you did not know. It has made her the best female commentator in the sport by a long shot—and one of the best in the whole business.

As the years went by we talked occasionally and I was assigned to do several instructional articles with her for *Golf Digest*. En route to one picture-taking session, during the JCPenney Classic in Florida, I took her on an adventurous ride over and around cart paths that she still talks about. Another famous golfer with whom I collaborated, the late teaching professional Davis Love Jr., once swore off ever driving with me after a similarly hairy experience. But Judy did not abandon me. In fact, I was delighted when I was approached to help her with this project. I doubt many TV commentators would have made that choice, given my role as a frequent critic of same for *Golf Digest*.

Her competitive career predated my involvement in covering the game. But the record shows she was one of the best of her era and one of the greatest players in LPGA Tour history. She began at an extraordinarily young age, 15, when she played in her first U.S. Women's Open in 1960. She joined the LPGA two years later and went on to record 27 victories. In 1976, she won six times, including the prestigious Dinah Shore (although silly LPGA rules don't retroactively count it as a major victory) and became the first woman in history to surpass the $100,000 mark in earnings for a season. Back problems cut her career short in the early 1980s, a few wins shy of the magical 30 required for entry into the LPGA Hall of Fame. But more than a few people—Nancy Lopez among them—consider her a Hall of Famer. She did it all despite being relatively short and light, and with two personal trademarks—a "strong" left-hand grip that was ahead of its time, and a hair band that she wore because she didn't like hats. She still has the grip—and many of the top players in the game have adopted similar ones since—but she has thankfully lost the hair band. She was also a pioneer in being the first prominent woman pro to raise a family—son Tuey is now a football coach— while continuing her career.

Judy would be the first to admit she has undergone a transformation. As a player she was so determined, so intent on success that the warmth she displays today in person and on television did not often come across. She jokes about how people thought she was so "mean." Since she got into TV, she has lost much of that edge and become a very engaging personality, as well as an astute commentator.

She has two nicknames, "Pro Talker" and, my personal favorite, "Fairway Bird." The latter derives from a British Open, when a spectator saw her on the course working for ABC and proclaimed, "Look, there's a bird out on the fairway." Bird is slang for woman in British parlance, as in "chatting up the birds" in a pub. I think you get the idea. Anyway, Judy was more flattered than offended. She has been a role model for women in golf most of her life, but she's done it quietly. She transcends her gender—Judy remains the only female announcer regularly assigned to PGA Tour events at the network level—and is widely respected by the pros on both tours. I'm sure this is why so many of them were happy to cooperate in contributing their insights for this book.

This project took nearly a year from conception to completion and included several lengthy sessions with Judy to research and go over the material, from Turnberry, Scotland, to Tampa, Florida, and from Hilton Head, South Carolina, to Dallas (twice). She was very hands-on throughout the entire project in making sure the words were precise and accurate. Because of her television work, she expresses herself succinctly and with great clarity, and that made my job in transferring her thoughts to paper a lot easier. I appreciated her insistence on being involved in every aspect to make sure it all came out just right. I hope it has.

I've enjoyed getting to know Judy and learning more about golf by talking and listening to her. I know you will too.

—Peter McCleery
Trumbull, Connecticut
May 1995

INTRODUCTION

I began playing golf as a little girl of six, introduced to the game by my father. I believe this early start was of tremendous benefit in the success I was able to achieve, and I always encourage people to expose children to the game early on. This ingrains an affinity for the fundamentals—the mechanics, rhythm, touch, feel, and etiquette—all the elements that go into making golf such a highly challenging, at times frustrating, but always wonderful game. Even if you do not take it too seriously, that experience and familiarity will serve you well later should you come back to it, as many adults do. Conversely, the later you begin, the harder—and more frustrating—it seems to be.

Young people can mimic so easily—they never dream of being self-conscious—so that between televised golf and the availability of video, if you show them enough good swings and good players, they will naturally absorb a lot. A longtime friend of mine and outstanding amateur player, Helen Sigel Wilson, has an interesting theory: If you let children see only *good players*, they would all have good swings!

Golf is a difficult game for everyone, particularly for beginners and especially for women. It's hard to learn. It's an awkward game, the courses are very difficult, and I can understand why women feel intimidated by people who play better and are stronger. But maybe you perceive it as being tougher than it actually is. I hope this book will address those issues and make the game more enjoyable and inviting.

Recent statistics from the National Golf Foundation show a tremendous upsurge in interest in the game among women. Nearly half of the new golfers coming into the game are women. That's the good news. The bad news is that, within a year, half of those women are giving up and leaving the game. I hope this book will help sustain and retain some of those would-be defectors. My goal is to help people play better, and to encourage those who are just starting to keep playing.

My career has spanned many levels of the game—from junior to amateur to professional, as a player and now as a broadcaster and a teacher. I don't claim to be an expert in everything, but I have observed, experienced, and

Recognize these two golfers? I first met LPGA legend Patty Berg when I was seven and she came to do a clinic and exhibition at the Triple A Golf Club in St. Louis.

Sometimes I think my golf swing was never better than when I was seven years old. Look at that extension! Oh, the beauty of youth—and the importance of getting an early start in this game.

learned a lot from many people over the years, and I will be passing along much of that knowledge in these pages. I've also enlisted some friends—ABC colleagues and players from the LPGA, Senior, and regular PGA Tour—to lend a tip or two that they think might help women golfers with what is undoubtedly the biggest obstacle they face: the inability to generate sufficient distance. Since so many women golfers, professionals included, spend most of their lives looking for 10 more yards, I thought we could use all the help we could get on this subject! These people have also contributed other tips and insights to help improve your game, and their comments are sprinkled throughout these pages. It's quite a collection of talent and knowledge, and I thank them here for their input.

I also hope golf course designers and course managers will take another look at how they set up golf courses for women. I believe that most women—the recreational players—are playing courses on which they have very little

With my father, Paul, in 1952 as I got my first pair of golf shoes. I was off!

With Bob Green, the pro at Triple A Golf Club in St. Louis—another early mentor

My son, Tuey, playing in the Hall of Fame pro-am at Pinehurst in 1978. He was a good little player and still loves the game today.

chance of reaching the majority of the greens in regulation. Even good players are playing regulation courses where, if they play their normal game, they reach only a handful of greens in regulation figures. Maybe we need to take a more realistic look at yardages and par for women. As a little girl, I remember my father used to give me a personal par for each hole—a realistic number for me to shoot for, not necessarily what was on the scorecard. A long par 5 would become a par 6 for me, because there was no way I could get to the green, even with my three best shots. I'll share some of these kinds of

In the ABC golf commentary booth.

thoughts, adjustments, and suggestions for making the game more fun as you get into it and as you get better.

A big part of this game is mental—about coping with adversity. Golf is not about what goes right. The game is very much about coping with and making something good out of things that go wrong. The only real constant is that the ball is round—you hope. The weather is different, the golf course is different, and you are different every day. It's not an exact science every time you tee it up by any means. But sometimes I think women golfers need to adopt a more aggressive, risk-taking approach. I see amateurs who are too careful for fear of making a mistake, because it is so hard to recover. I don't think it's much fun playing that way, and we'll pass along some thoughts about how a change in your mental approach can pay dividends.

Working as an "on-course commentator" for ABC since 1984, I've had a privileged view of professional golf for the past dozen years, walking inside the ropes and watching the best players in the world. I wasn't trying to be a trailblazer, but I'm grateful for the opportunity to cover both men's and women's golf. Some people have questioned whether a woman can relate to the man's game. I've tried to offer an honest perspective. I know it's taught me a few things about how we all can approach the game and certain situations differently. I sure wish I had this experience back when I was playing in the 1960s and 1970s, because I've learned so much. But I will try to pass along that knowledge of the men and women professionals.

While I'm targeting women golfers as the main audience, the majority of my thoughts are equally applicable to men. Golf is golf, and my instructional theories have been molded by many men I've come in contact with over the years. It's been said many times that male golfers would be better off trying to emulate the top women golfers, since they share with women a similar ability to create clubhead speed, more than they do with, say, John Daly and Greg Norman.

All golfers, men and women, professional and amateur, are united by one thing: their desire to improve. That's one of the great things about playing, or teaching, or doing television—you're always learning how to get better.

I hope this book will help you to do that.

1

OVERCOMING THE INTIMIDATION FACTOR

So you decide you want to play golf. You buy a set of clubs, get a tee time, put on a golf outfit, and go to the course. Ready, aim, fire away. This is going to be fun, right? Well, maybe that's the wrong approach, especially at the beginning.

Golf is a game that requires a gentle, maybe even a calculated, start. Anybody who tells you to just go get the equipment and run out to your nearest course, and you will instantly love this game is probably wrong. It definitely helps to kind of "sneak up" on it, building confidence and success very gradually before making a full frontal assault on a golf course. It's not like being thrown in a swimming pool and finding you can swim.

I began at age six, in the wintertime, hitting balls at an indoor driving range. I was taught to swing the club by my father and a St. Louis golf pro, Bob Green. They put my hands on the club pretty much right and got me standing up to the ball correctly. Then I was allowed only to take the club back a foot and through a foot. I just kind of bumped the ball off the tee with a 7-iron. After I did that for a short time, a few weeks or so, they would have me take it another foot farther back. At the end of these sessions, my father would always "treat" me by letting me take one swing as big and as hard as I could. But that was it. Everything else was in mini-steps.

It took more than three months before I developed something resembling a full golf swing. It turned out to be a very good way to learn, because I didn't develop a lot of bad habits. My mechanics were pretty correct from the beginning. Most people today lack the patience to learn to play this way. They want to get out there and have at it. But if they'd try a similar method, it would be well worth their while. When you actually get out to the course, you'll have a better foundation, and you won't get nearly as discouraged as some beginners do.

A Gentle Approach

Tread softly in the beginning and find a comfort level. When you do take your game to the golf course the first couple of times, try to pick a time (probably in the early morning, late afternoon, or evening) when it isn't crowded and you won't have to worry about holding other players up. You can play nine holes or less, to get a feel for the game and the course and what it takes. Avoid putting yourself under so much pressure in the beginning that you will be embarrassed or nervous and end up not wanting to go back. Leave yourself wanting more. Be realistic. If you've hit balls only three times in your life and someone says, "Let's go play golf," you still may not be ready. You cannot possibly cope with playing 18 holes and all that goes with it. For one thing, you don't have the time. This could be an eight-hour experience. You don't want to do this.

Why do so many women golfers leave the game so soon after taking it up? I believe many of them have gone to the golf course before they are really ready. There is a lot of fun in hitting practice balls, particularly if you find you are making some progress. In the beginning, that should be your entrée to the game. I'd recommend also chipping and spending time on the practice putting green. Bob Toski, who taught me a great deal in my early years as a professional, talks about how "small success patterns" build bigger ones. The putting green is the place to start building success by getting a feel for the stroke and distance control.

Being exposed and introduced to the game through someone with experience can really help. Some of the people who get discouraged and quit have never had a real lesson. It is wise for beginners to take a lesson from a trained teaching professional before they get out there. I'll have more to say on taking lessons later.

In lieu of lessons from a professional, it's nice to get started through someone who plays pretty well. This works best if he or she has a special talent for communicating—and some patience. A friend can take you out to the range or the course in the evening to play a few holes. You need someone who will do this through the early stages of development and provide plenty of encouragement along the way.

Most beginners play together, which is fine, but you have to reach farther to improve. If not, you stagnate. Playing with people who are better than you helps you to become a better player. If you are always playing with people who are *worse* than you are, you might not find the game a whole lot of fun.

Back at my home club in Midland, Texas, a group of good players organized a tournament for beginners. Four of us invited 16 other women who were not as advanced to play a scramble format. Everyone hit the tee shot, we picked the best one, and all hit our next shot from there; we did the same thing until we holed out. You can impose rules, like requiring each group to use every player's tee shot at least two or three times. This gets everyone involved—and having some fun and some success in participating. It is something any women's group could do, but the key is making sure the rank beginners integrate with the better players occasionally.

Getting Serious

Competition is a big part of the game's appeal. There's competition with yourself, to lower your handicap, and there's competition to beat other people. I think golf tends to be more social with women, some of whom avoid serious competition. Men are different that way. They can have a 40 handicap and they'll still get out there with a big wager. Play for a little something. You can have a contest among your group to see who puts the ball in the fairway the most on all the non-par-3 holes, or who has the fewest putts, something simple. There should be some stake involved, whether it's $1 or lunch.

You should definitely establish a handicap as soon as you can. It shows you're serious about the game. A lot of the fun of golf is improving, and a handicap index shows you in stark terms where you stand. Anything under 30 —meaning you might have a chance to break 100 for 18 holes —is above average for a woman golfer. You need to see how a handicap works and allows people of all different playing levels to play together and against each other.

Playing Matches

Once you have a handicap, you can play with anyone. By getting or giving your opponent an agreed-upon number of "strokes," you can still have a competitive match. That's how most club matches are played. The most popular format is best-ball. You see it in team events such as the Ryder Cup and Solheim Cup for pros, and the Curtis and Walker Cup matches for the best amateurs. Two players take on another two, with you and your partner picking the best score per hole. Whichever team has the lower score on that hole wins it. The team that has won the most holes after nine or 18 wins the match. These sorts of games can create some great friendships and

rivalries. There are endless variations on games and formats that you can explore as you get more and more involved.

Early Exposure

I think the real key for parents and their children is early exposure. School programs tend to expose kids to team sports such as soccer and basketball. But there's something special, too, about individual sports. Some people are fortunate to live near a course or have parents who introduce them to the game. But exposure to golf is not automatic for many. The LPGA and PGA tours are both doing a lot to bring more people into the game. I encourage people to send their daughters and sons to junior clinics. Some will gravitate to other games, but a good number of them will end up in golf for the rest of their lives. And even those who do not take to it right away can always come back to it. I see many young mothers who want to take up the game after their children have reached school age. Many say, "I haven't really played golf, but I played a little bit in high school with my dad and I took a golf class in college." Even people with that little bit of golf experience will have a big advantage later.

When you think about it, of all the sports that we all love to watch and become involved in, golf is the only one that you can do as a child, play as an adult, and then play with your grandchildren. If you're starting late, make sure your kids get an earlier start on this one-of-a-kind game of a lifetime.

2

BEGINNING FOR BEGINNERS

The 7-Iron, 30-Day Test

I see so many women in their 40s and 50s who have decided to take up golf. Their children are in school or out of the house and they finally have the time to play. So they go buy clubs, balls, shoes—the whole nine yards. After one summer, you never see them again.

If you are just taking up golf, you need to begin a little more slowly. You don't need to start out with a full set of clubs. One or two clubs will do. For true beginners, I find a 7-iron is a great club, because it's long enough to give you the feel of swinging and has enough loft to get the ball up in the air and get you hitting full shots. That should be your introductory club. Don't hit drivers or wedges right away. A driver is the longest club and, in many ways, the toughest to control. A wedge has a whole different look to it—it's a very heavy club, and is also the shortest club in the bag.

I recommend that, before you attack this game in earnest, you undergo a "7-iron, 30-day" trial period. You can find a club in an old-club barrel. You don't even need golf shoes to start with—sneakers are fine. But what you need to do is spend a month or so with that 7-iron to find out if you want to go any further. I believe such a gentle start is far more encouraging than attacking the game all-out.

You'll need to develop the physical strength to play golf. It requires muscles you may not be used to using. The best way to do that is by hitting balls. Ideally, you should get an introductory lesson before you start.

Getting a Grip

When you try to put your hands on the golf club it will feel very awkward at first. See Chapter 3 for the basic grip that I recommend. Once you get your

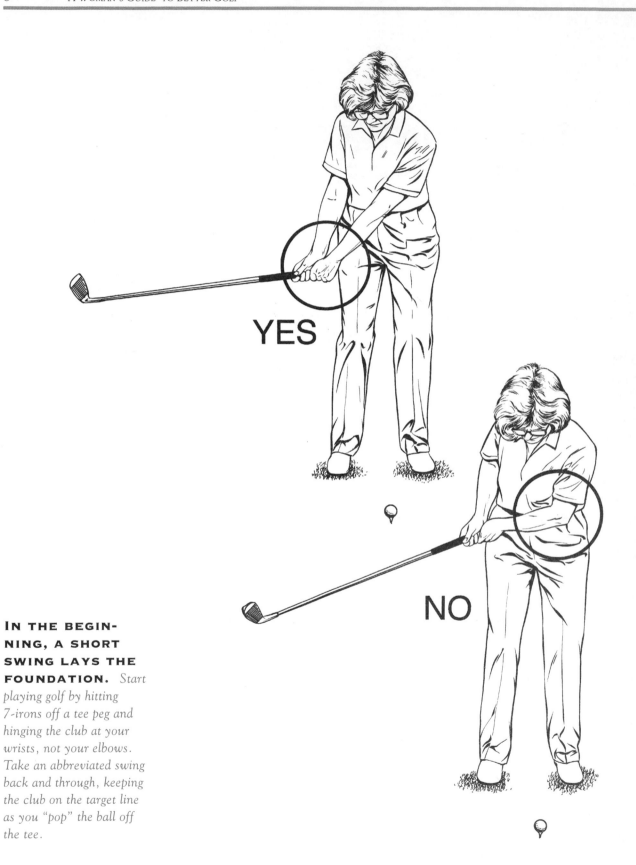

YES

NO

**IN THE BEGIN-
NING, A SHORT
SWING LAYS THE
FOUNDATION.** *Start
playing golf by hitting
7-irons off a tee peg and
hinging the club at your
wrists, not your elbows.
Take an abbreviated swing
back and through, keeping
the club on the target line
as you "pop" the ball off
the tee.*

SWING ON A PATH TOWARD YOUR TARGET. *Imagine a dotted line through the ball to the target and the club traveling on that line to the target.*

hands on the club correctly, it's time to hit a few balls. Always put the ball on a tee when you're beginning, your feet set apart about shoulder width, and the ball forward in your stance, in line with your left heel. If you have never hit balls before, you'll tend to swing the club like an ax. Having the ball too far back in your stance, toward your right foot, will encourage you to be a chopper.

Make a Short Swing

Don't try to hit the ball too hard. Take the club a couple of feet back and through the ball, just as my father taught me. Feel the sensation of the club-face meeting the ball solidly.

It's best to get a feel for this game by hitting balls somewhere on a practice range before you get your baptism of fire on a golf course.

The biggest key to making the club return to the ball is to keep the left arm comfortably extended at the start and throughout your backswing. This returns you to the ball at the same position you were at address, so you can hit the back of the ball. By taking an abbreviated, two- or three-foot swing to start, you won't hinge at the left elbow as many beginners do. And don't try to hit the ball very far.

The part of your arm that does have a little "give" or break is your wrist. Your left wrist should break above your thumb. We want wrist hinging, not elbow hinging here, and we want simply to "pop" the ball off the tee. It is very important that you swing the club on a path toward your target. Imagine a dotted line through the ball to the target and the club traveling on the line to the target for a short way, maybe six inches, after impact. If you think of your right hand and arm as throwing a ball underhanded to the target, swinging to that target will become more natural.

You're going to be hitting the ball only between 30 and 50 yards, but that's OK. Over a 30-day period, work your way up to a three-quarters swing, swinging your hands and arms up to shoulder height. You're giving yourself a reasonable chance of knowing if you have any affinity for this game. If you decide you like what you've seen, you're ready to move on, adding a few clubs, maybe playing a few holes. Build success from the ground up, and build a sound foundation from which to progress.

The Basics

In the ensuing chapters we will detail more of the basic instruction you'll need. But these elements will be critical:

- **Good posture,** with your knees flexed and standing a comfortable distance from the ball so that your weight is balanced from the balls of your feet to your heels. Most beginners tend to stand either too far forward on their toes or back on their heels.

- **Balance.** Try to feel as if you're light on your feet, much like a good dancer, not as if you're "nailed" to the ground. Good balance allows freedom of movement.

- **Grip pressure.** Feel as though you have control of the club but not a death grip on it. Have a nice, firm, comfortable grip, without a lot of pressure and tension. I shouldn't be able to take the club from your hands. You have control of it, but you are not squeezing it hard or holding on to it for dear life. You don't want to feel your hands and wrists and forearm muscles tightening, since a certain tightening of the grip occurs naturally near impact.

Beginners tend to grip the club so tightly or in such a poor way that the club moves in their hands. If you check your grip and your grip pressure, I think you can overcome it. A little salt water can cure your first blister and you can go back out and hit balls the next day.

Alternating with your 7-iron, you might also spend a little time with a putter and getting a feel for the stroke, which is a miniature version of the full golf swing. Start with short putts and work your way outward. Get a feel for distance and the different length of stroke required to get the ball to

roll the right amount. A putt of two feet, for example, requires a back stroke of only about four inches. A lot of beginners might have played miniature golf, and this part of the game will be somewhat familiar to them already. See Chapter 6 for a good deal more about putting.

Throughout this book, I will bring up certain theories and techniques that may not apply to beginners—for example, various wedge shots or bunker shots that are really for better, more advanced players. As you progress and stay with this game, you can come back and try them. At some point, they will mean more to you.

For now, I think it's important to begin with those little 7-iron shots. If I could start most people this way, I'm convinced that a good percentage of them would go on. And now we will go on—to talk about the grip and other fundamentals.

3

THE GRIP

Getting Your Hands on the Club Correctly

Your hands are your only contact with the golf club. That's why a good, functional grip is so very important. The right grip promotes a sense of "feel." As one becomes more advanced, there is a great sense of communication between the golf club and the player's hands. To help you understand the information in this chapter, you should know that having either the left or right hand turned more to your left is considered a "weaker" position; having either hand turned to the right is a "stronger" grip. Having both thumbs straight up and down the shaft is the most neutral position.

The "strong" grip has been closely associated with me for as long as I can remember. When I arrived on the LPGA Tour in the early 1960s, no one had ever seen anything like it. My left hand was turned far more to the right than was considered conventional or even acceptable. Marlene Hagge was at the height of her career in the '60s, with a semi-strong left-hand grip. She was an exceptional ball-striker and had a right-to-left shot to be envied. Donna Caponi came along with a very strong grip and had an illustrious career, including back-to-back U.S. Women's Opens. But my grip was slightly more exaggerated and the one people always talked about. Many of the "experts" bet I could never win with it. A lot of people considered it a "caddie" grip. Not so much anymore!

Today, a so-called strong grip is much more in favor, even among the game's very best players. Paul Azinger, Fred Couples, Bernhard Langer, 1995 British Open champion John Daly, and Rookie of the Year David Duval among the men, and Laura Davies, Nancy Lopez, and young Kelly Robbins on the LPGA Tour are all members of the club now. The stigma once associated with a strong grip has been removed. I feel that I've been vindicated. In fact, grips among a lot of well-known golfers are getting stronger.

What was once termed an "orthodox" grip is now considered weak. Jack Nicklaus, for example, has moved his left hand into a slightly stronger position in recent years, as he tries to maintain his ability to generate clubhead speed as he gets older.

The Rankin Grip Is Born

I started playing as a youngster with a standard left-hand position on the club. But I soon encountered a problem that happens more often with women than men, and that was that the inside of my left elbow would point up in the air at address. My father and other people who helped me tried to get the back of that left elbow pointing more at the target. I discovered that by turning my left hand more to the right, I could make the back of my left elbow point at the target. You find a way to make accommodations, and my left-hand grip became very strong in trying to change my left-elbow position. I immediately began to hit the ball farther. Throughout the years, many people thought I would—or should—change it, but I never did. If anything, it became even stronger as the years went by. It became known, in some circles, as "the Rankin Grip."

I have always believed this grip makes tremendous sense, especially for weaker players and women. In fact, I would defy anyone to find what could be termed a "weak" grip on the LPGA Tour today. It is a very natural way to grip a golf club. Here's why: If you just let your arms hang freely at your sides, chances are your palms don't turn in against the body. For most of us, the palms are turned more inward and/or behind us, with the tops of our hands facing forward. If you go from that position to lifting your arms to grip a golf club, the left hand will be in a naturally "strong" starting position.

The Benefits of a Strong Left Hand

Very few amateur golfers need help because they hook the ball. Ninety percent slice their shots. When I was learning the game, people believed that golf was a left-sided game played by right-handed golfers. Today, there has been some revisionist thinking on this. But it never made sense to me to take the left hand of a right-handed golfer and put it on the club in the weakest position possible. If we are trying to get our left side equal to our right in strength and feel, then a strong left-hand grip simply makes sense. Golfers with strong left-hand grips tend to make solid contact with the ball—and that is

When you hang your arms at your sides, your palms will most likely be facing behind you. They don't face your body unless your arms turn outward. From my palms' position, if you were to lift your hands and lay them on a golf club, it would be in a reasonably "strong" position without any twisting and turning. That's why I contend that my grip is a natural for most people.

one of the keys to developing consistency. You're not going to hit as many bad shots when you hit the ball right on the nose. You will also find that these players tend to be very good in the wind, because of their ability to hit the ball flush.

Another plus is that a strong left hand puts you in a preset position to cock your hands later in the swing. With a more orthodox grip, a certain amount of forearm rotation is required to achieve that position. So we have eliminated a moving part in the swing with a strong grip—which should make for a more accurate player.

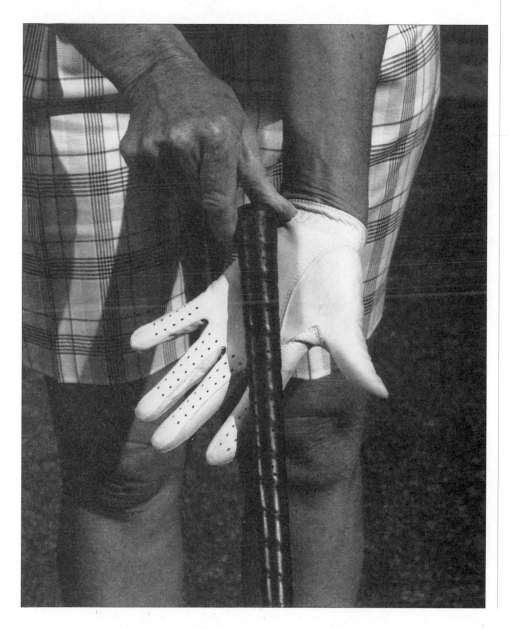

DIAGONALLY ACROSS THE LEFT PALM. *To put your hands on a golf club, start with your left hand (if you're a right-handed player). The club should be gripped diagonally across the palm in your left hand. The grip is across the base of the fingers, really more in the palm than in the fingers themselves. The last three fingers are the controlling parts of your left-hand grip, and your left thumb should go on last and be on the right-hand side of the grip.*

In getting started, it might help to draw a diagonal line across your golf glove that shows where you should grip the club in your left hand.

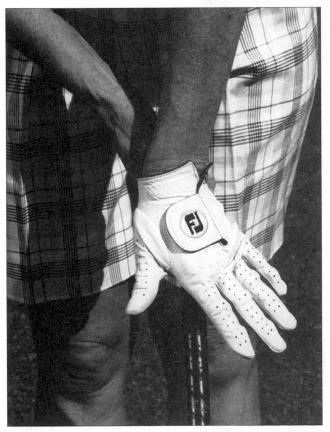

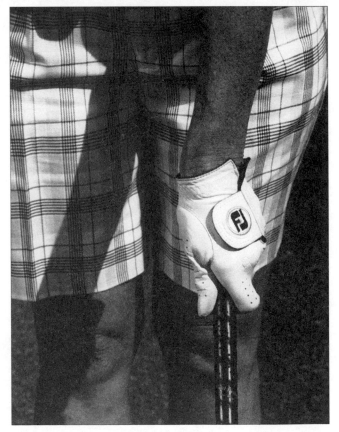

LEFT-HAND GRIP. *Here is my left-hand grip with the fingers opened—before I have closed them around the grip on the club—and after I close them. Notice how the left thumb sticks down by itself on the right side of the club.*

THE "V" TEST. *With what is considered an orthodox, or standard, grip, the "V" formed by the thumb and forefinger points at your chin.*

With a strong grip like mine, the left hand turns clockwise to the right so that the "V" goes to the right of your chin or to your right shoulder. Mine goes even outside my right shoulder.

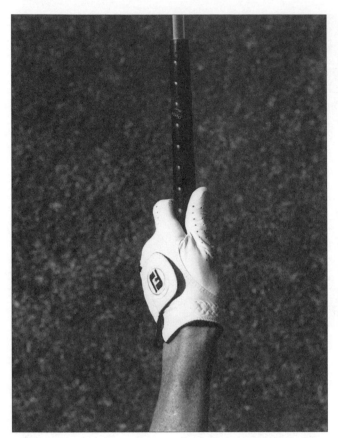

Looking over my shoulder at the grip, you see the same thing from another angle. The left-hand grip is often referred to in terms of how many knuckles are visible. With the more conventional grip (shown here), you can really see only the knuckle on the left forefinger.

When the left hand is turned to the right, as many as three or even all four knuckles become visible.

The "V" Test

The simplest way to check your left-hand grip is by checking the direction of the "V" formed between your thumb and left forefinger when placed on the club. With a strictly orthodox or "neutral" grip, that "V" points almost at your chin. (You will rarely see a grip this weak in the left hand today.) When your grip starts to get stronger—turned clockwise to the right—the "V" goes to the right of your chin and, in some cases, to the right shoulder. Mine even goes outside my right shoulder. But I think toward the right shoulder is a good place to have your "V" pointing.

If this inspires you to go from an orthodox grip to a stronger one, you may want to do it gradually. Give yourself time to adapt. Move your left hand to

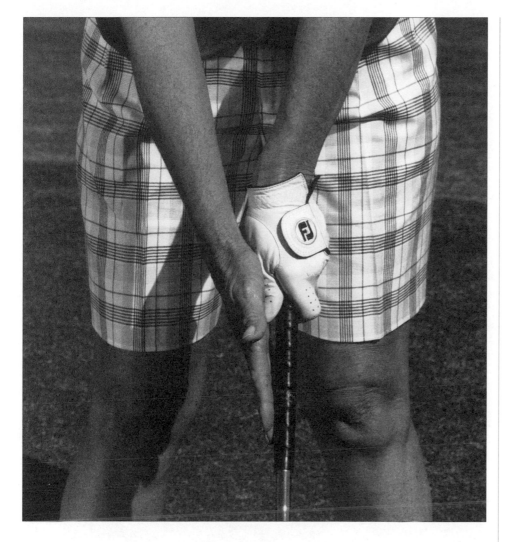

APPLYING THE RIGHT HAND. *Whether you have a strong, orthodox, or weaker left-hand grip, the idea is for your two hands to fit together on the golf club. Your hands should work together as one. Here I'm beginning to apply my right hand against my left, with the fingers extended and my palm directly facing the target. There is a valley that runs down your palm, and that valley in your right hand provides a perfect fit for your left thumb.*

the right in small increments, working toward your right shoulder, until you have a finished product you're happy with.

The Right Hand

A good right-hand grip is a necessary adjunct to a strong left-hand grip. With your right hand, your goal is to create a snug fit with your left—with your right palm facing the target. Trying to teach someone a sense of feel for what the clubface is doing is oftentimes very difficult. Having the right palm face the target is one of those "little things" that can help you develop a greater sense of feel for what the clubface is doing in the swing.

THE PISTOL GRIP PROVIDES FEEL. *With the right-hand grip, the thumb and forefinger are the controlling fingers. I am very much in favor of the "pistol" grip—you separate the right forefinger and put it and your right thumb in a pistol-like position. This imparts a greater sense of feel and direction for what the club is doing.*

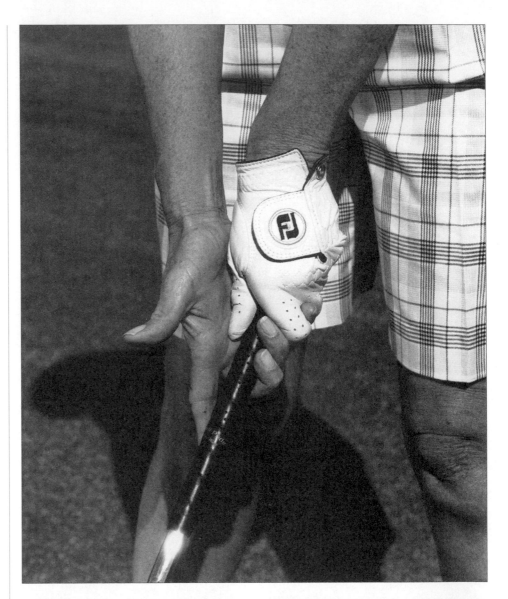

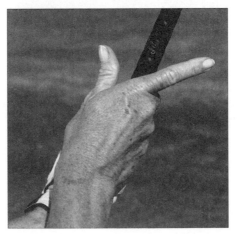

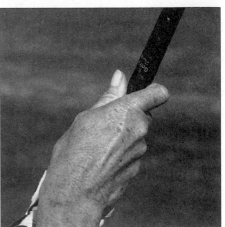

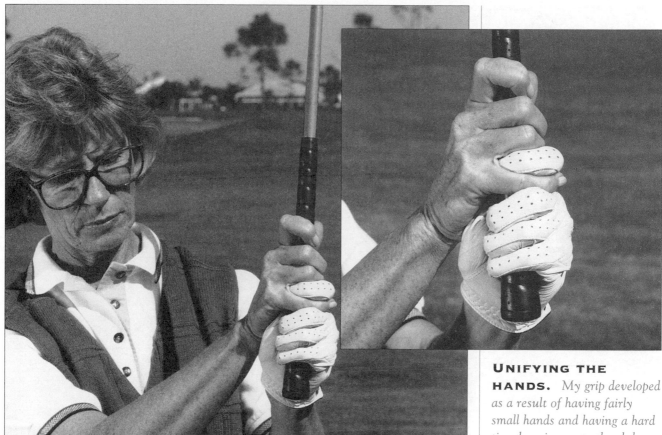

Whether you have a strong grip or a more neutral one, you do not want the two hands to ever oppose each other. You do *not* want a strong left hand and a weak right hand or a strong left hand and an even stronger right hand. Your two hands have to fit together, because the ideal in swinging a club and hitting a golf ball is for your hands to work together as one. And you are trying to return your hands at impact—the moment of truth when club meets ball—to the way you started at address.

The left-hand grip is more of a full-handed grip. The club should lie diagonally across the palm of your hand before the fingers wrap around the grip end of the club. The right hand's position is then molded around the left thumb. The left thumb fits into the valley formed by your right palm. When you put your right hand on the club, it tends to be more in the fingers. The last three fingers of your left hand are the controlling fingers. With your right hand, control rests in the other two digits—your thumb and forefinger. The

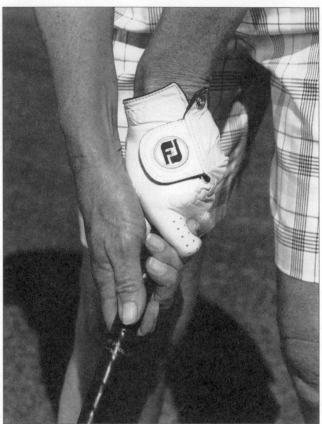

THE COMPLETED PICTURE. *Here are three views of what my finished grip looks like. Note how the strong left hand is now united with the right hand and how the right thumb and forefinger have stayed in the "pistol" position.*

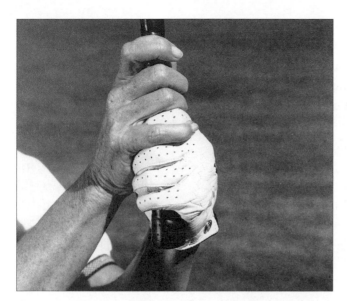

OVERLAPPING GRIP. *There are several popular variations on how to unify the two hands. The basic "overlapping" grip has the little finger of the right hand riding on top of the second and third fingers of the left hand. This is known as the Vardon grip, named for the turn-of-the-century British professional who first advocated it.*

INTERLOCKING GRIP. *People with smaller hands often prefer to "interlock" their little finger, slipping it between the forefinger and middle finger of the left hand. The left forefinger then pulls out and touches against the last knuckle of the right hand. Jack Nicklaus is the most famous proponent of the interlocking grip.*

OVERLOCKING GRIP. *My grip is kind of a hybrid, with the little finger of my right hand riding between those same two fingers on my left hand. However, I don't pull the left forefinger out. That's the difference between my grip and the interlock. It's somewhere between overlapping and interlocking, so I call it the overlocking grip.*

TEN-FINGER GRIP. *Another option, used successfully by many women, is the 10-finger grip, also known as the baseball grip. All 10 fingers of the two hands touch the grip of the club—there is no overlocking, interlocking, or overlapping. This is a good "starter" grip, because many people are used to holding other objects— like a baseball bat—in this way. Beth Daniel is the best-known player who uses a 10-finger grip.*

little finger of your right hand overlaps the index finger of your left in an over-lapping grip.

I favor putting the first two fingers of the right hand in the form of a "pistol" grip, as the photographs show. Using the thumb and forefinger in this fashion gives a player a lot of extra feel and sense for what the club is doing. It's one of those little things that a lot of players probably aren't even aware of—but that good players do.

The two hands can be united in a variety of ways. I have fairly long fingers, which gives me more leeway in how I grip a club. If you have short fingers and small hands, your options are somewhat limited. The interlocking and 10-finger grips are more successful for people with small hands. The traditional overlapping grip seems to require some finger length to feel secure. The various grip options are shown on page 21.

COMMON FLAW: People who are comfortable with a strong left-hand grip often get their right hand too far underneath the club, turned to the right. This leaves a big gap between your two hands. Fit your right hand as closely as you can to your left. In the best of strong grips, the left thumb is not visible.

Take plenty of time as you get started to get a grip you are comfortable with and that is technically correct. This is your only direct link to the golf club, and your grip will have tremendous influence on the degree of success you are able to achieve. There are any number of bad grips that we have not even discussed—and it is very difficult to be any good when your grip isn't.

4

GETTING READY

Posture, Address, and Alignment

I n this chapter we are going to discuss some of the things you need to do correctly before you start to swing the club: posture, address, and alignment of the feet and clubface.

Posture

One of the things that a golfer should have is the athletic-ready posture that you would take for a lot of other activities, like doing aerobic exercises, shooting a basketball, or swinging a baseball bat. What we're looking for is a position from which our weight can move back and forth, and yet still allows for balance. Balance is the key here. The one factor every athletic and dance activity shares is balance. What we're ultimately striving for in golf is to have freedom of movement and great balance in the swing. That's the ideal. People who are afraid of movement or are taking the idea of "swinging in a barrel" to extremes—with their feet stuck to the floor—are not going to achieve it. Don't be that rigid.

You want to stand up to the ball in a comfortable posture, with your left arm comfortably extended and your knees flexed. Your weight should be more toward the middle of your feet, from the balls of your feet to your heels, definitely not on your toes. Good posture has your backside out and your back relatively straight—not ramrod straight, but relatively straight. I recommend this for everybody. In the case of women, it allows us more freedom to swing our arms around our bodies. The overall sensation at address should be one of readiness and stability.

You want to bend to the ball where your legs meet your body. Too often, people bend at the waist to get to the ball. That's not right. Bend at your *hip joints*, where your legs meet your body. I have somewhat of a hard time doing this because it causes stress on my back. I have accommodated this by bend-

PROPER POSTURE. *Good posture begins with an athletic-ready position—bent at your hip joints where your legs meet your body, and with your knees flexed (1). Comfortably extend your left arm to the ball to find the correct distance from the ball at address (2). Notice that here (3) I have bent at the hips and flexed my knees. This position (4) allows my back to stay relatively straight—not ramrod straight, but reasonably straight. Back straight with backside sticking out is the preferred address position. You need to keep your chin pointed up (5), not too far down in your chest. Here I am (6 and 7) all finished with my address and ready to go, from the down-the-line and face-on angles.*

DAVE STOCKTON, JR.

Won $185,205 in 1994,
rookie season on PGA Tour

"This is some-
thing my dad be-
lieves and I do,
too. Many women are almost
double-jointed—they can put
their arms out and touch their
elbows together. Most men
can't do this. Unfortunately,
this flexibility has a negative
effect in how women set up to
play golf.

"They tend to have their
arms too close together, with
the inside of their arms pointing up, toward the sky. They
need to relax their arms and
point the left elbow toward the
target; that will push the right
arm out so that it can relax underneath the left. This starting position doesn't come
naturally to most women, but
they can and should do it.
They'll make a better takeaway, and it also prevents their
elbows from breaking down on
the backswing. They'll be able
to extend their left arm and
maintain better control of the
club throughout the swing,
producing more power."

ing in my upper back, which is not the best way to do it. Everybody is different and has different problems that must be addressed. But the best posture to create for ease in swinging a golf club is with your fanny out and your back comfortably straight.

Another misleading term is "bending your knees." What we want is for you to *flex* your knees—again, to get in an athletic position where you are going to have balance and freedom of movement at the same time. Bending your knees very deeply restricts your movement and in effect makes you shorter. Unless you are a pretty tall woman, you probably do not need to be shorter hitting a golf ball. Flexing your knees, creating just a slight "give" at the joint area, gives you freedom. So don't think *bend*—think *flex*.

Because the right hand sits farther down the shaft than the left, the right shoulder will be lower than the left. This is important, but not something you want to exaggerate. If you allow your right side to relax naturally from the outset, it will automatically be lower than your left. It is a simple physical fact. If you find that your right side is too high at address with the arm fully extended, it's a sign that you are probably standing too far from the ball. At address, the left arm is extended and the right arm is relaxed. If the right arm is extended and tense, there is a flaw in your address position.

Ball Position

Ball position is what I call an "absolute fundamental," because if it is incorrect, it will create flaws in your swing. A common mistake is playing the ball too far back in your stance and aiming too far to the right. This leads to all kinds of problems. I try to simplify my ball position by using my left foot and the center of my stance as reference points. As the clubs get longer, my stance gets wider and I stand farther away from the ball. With shorter irons, I'm standing closer to the ball and my right foot moves closer to my left. But the ball position really does not move that far in relation to the center of my stance—only about four inches or so. The more often you can hit the ball from the same position, the better chance you have of making consistently solid contact.

With a driver, I like to play the ball pretty far forward, on the inside of my left toe. This is because the ball is teed, and also because I'm a "sweeper": With my driver and most of my long clubs, I try to sweep the ball toward the target with the sole of the clubhead moving parallel to the ground at the moment of impact.

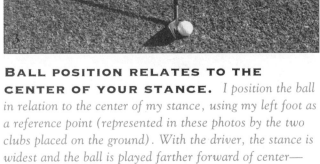

BALL POSITION RELATES TO THE CENTER OF YOUR STANCE. *I position the ball in relation to the center of my stance, using my left foot as a reference point (represented in these photos by the two clubs placed on the ground). With the driver, the stance is widest and the ball is played farther forward of center—*

between my left toe and heel (1). In the succeeding shots, the stance gradually narrows and the ball moves incrementally closer to the center of my stance. For a fairway wood (2), the ball is inside of my left heel; for a long iron (3) and middle iron (4), it has moved back slightly but remains well forward of center.

BALL POSITION (CONTINUED). *As the stance narrows for a short iron (5), the ball has moved near center, while a wedge (6) is played pretty much in the center of my stance. Let your hands fall naturally with every address position. Don't force them forward or back. There are very few specialty shots in which the ball is played back of center. The contrast between the driver position and the wedge position (7) reinforces the point that the ball has really not moved as much as people think—about four inches throughout this whole sequence.*

The ball moves just slightly back, off my left heel, for a fairway wood and just inside it for a long iron. It remains well left of center. Even for short irons and wedges, because the stance has narrowed so much, the ball position is still only toward the center of my stance. There are only a few unusual situations where you will ever want the ball back of center. The pictures accompanying this section will help to illustrate what I'm talking about. The ball really does not have to move around in your stance as much as people think.

Alignment

To get into position, I always approach the ball from behind, to get a sense of the intended line to my target. The target line is simply an imaginary line extending from your ball to the target you wish your ball to start on. I walk up to the ball from behind, and the first thing I do, standing slightly behind

FEET SHOULD BE PERPENDICULAR TO CLUBFACE. *This alignment illustration shows how, if you get your clubface aligned properly to your target, all you have to do is set your feet down in a line somewhat perpendicular to the clubface.*

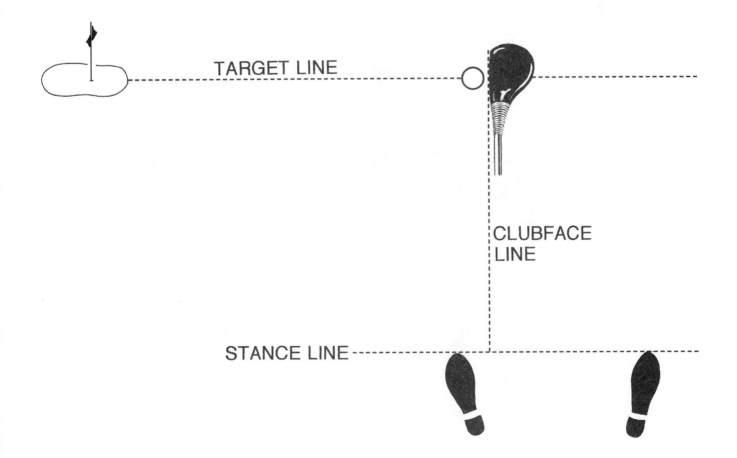

TARGET LINE

CLUBFACE LINE

STANCE LINE

GETTING INTO THE SHOT. *I always approach the ball from behind in order to see my target line clearly (1). I place and align the club along my target line first (2)* *and then move my feet into position (3 and 4). Get your club aligned properly and all you have to do is set your feet down in a somewhat perpendicular line to the clubface.*

the golf ball, is try to align the clubface to the target I have chosen. Then I place my left foot, which determines my ball position. My right foot is set last and determines the width of my stance.

I see a lot of people trying to get their feet right before they ever set the club down. Until the club is in position, you cannot determine your distance from the ball. It's imperative that the club is aligned first. Distance from the ball should be determined by a comfortable extension of your left arm—not a stiff, straight left arm and not a bent left arm, but one in which the left arm and club seem to be a straight line from the left shoulder to the clubhead.

I do not consciously try to set my feet parallel to my target line. I think it is much simpler to set your feet perpendicular to the line of the clubface. It is very difficult to look at the target and line up the clubface, then look back at the target and imagine aligning your feet in a parallel direction. It can become very confusing, and by the time you're ready to draw the club back, you are frozen. I believe that alignment should be kept as simple as possible. All you have to do is concentrate on setting your feet on a perpendicular line to the clubface—and the clubface should be aimed where you want the ball to go.

Your alignment may vary depending on the particular shot. For a wedge shot, you might be aiming right at the hole. Or you might be on the tee and trying to hit at the right center of the fairway. If you are hitting a 3-wood into the green and you have a right-to-left wind, you might be aiming 20 feet to the right of the flag. Align yourself with where you want the ball to start. That is not always the flagstick!

Here you see the same thing from behind the ball with a wood and an iron. The routine never changes, no matter what situation or club I have in my hand: I look toward the target from behind (1), align my clubface first (2), and then my feet (3).

Setting up for all of your shots in exactly the same way establishes a consistent pre-shot routine.

SPOT ALIGNMENT. *Some players like to "spot" align with a point positioned just slightly ahead of the ball by a foot or so. Whenever you see a player looking slightly ahead of the ball, as I am here, that is what he or she is doing. I have never used this technique myself, although many successful players have, including Jack Nicklaus.*

One of the most common mistakes made in golf is aiming to the right of the target. Our eyes are anywhere from six inches to a foot behind the ball, and it's a natural tendency. Ninety percent of all golfers who aim poorly, aim to the right. Aiming too far right encourages everything bad in a golf swing. It makes us pull the ball or come over the top—swinging down and across the ball rather than out through it. It causes slices. The better player who sets up a little bit to the right can draw the ball back into play. But the poorer player invariably tries to pull the ball back to the target.

Our subconscious is at work in golf, and our swing reacts to what we do in the setup. If you're a classic slicer, adjust your alignment correctly toward the line of the target; you'll be less inclined to swing across the ball with the clubface open. Forcing yourself to make this change is not always immediately successful, but stick with it and your shot pattern will improve.

Even tour players who work at the game seven days a week find that when they begin to fall into a slump, very often the culprit is a little change in their setup. It is amazing how our bodies—and, in turn, our swings—accommodate or adjust to little changes in our setup. When you take good players and re-

AT ADDRESS, YOUR STANCE IS EITHER SQUARE, OPEN, OR CLOSED IN RELATION TO TARGET LINE.
How you set your feet in relation to your target line will determine how the ball starts. The club on the ground here is pointing straight at my target and my feet are aligned perfectly parallel to that line, or "square," meaning I plan to hit the ball straight at the target.

Here my stance is slightly open, with the left foot dropped back from the target line. This position is for someone who favors hitting the ball from left to right (a fade).

Here my stance is closed, with the right foot dropped back from the target line. This is the setup for a player who likes to "draw" the ball, starting to the right and curving it back to the left.

turn them to their correct setup, their swing falls right back into place. How you approach the ball, set up to the ball, and how you get into position to start your golf swing have a lot to do with how well you are capable of swinging—and how often you can repeat those good swings.

Width of your feet

Your feet should be placed slightly wider apart than your shoulders. When you need to widen your stance more, move your right foot so you don't alter your ball position. Turn, or "flare," your feet slightly outward, since this will give you better balance and enable you to make a good body turn.

Setting up open, closed, or square

If you have a natural way that you work the ball—either a fade or a draw—groove that swing rather than trying to hit a straight ball, because the golfer who tries to hit it dead straight risks losing it either way. Many people believe that if you hit the ball from right to left—a draw—you are not going to be able to stop the ball as well. Unless your draw has turned into a nasty hook, I am not sure that is true. People who hit the ball right to left tend to hit the ball lower. Obviously, that ball is not going to stop as fast as the higher left-to-right shot. But I think if you can hit the ball high enough, you can turn it either way. In fact, a golf ball spins backward to gain height, regardless of the direction it curves at the end of the shot. A woman golfer who can't put much spin on the shot anyway is going to be better off hitting the shot right to left, because it is a stronger shot and will give her added length.

The position of your feet and shoulders at address will generally dictate your shot shape. In a nice square address position, your shoulders are ever so slightly open to the intended target line, simply because your left hand is higher on the club than your right. The tendency will be for your hands to return the clubhead along the target line through impact. It's best to align yourself so that your feet, legs, and hips are all pointing in the same direction.

COMMON FLAW: Watch that you don't get your shoulders too closed (aiming to the right), which makes it difficult to see your target.

The closing or opening of your stance involves aligning your entire body to one side of the target line. It is not simply a matter of positioning your feet. For example, pulling your left foot back away from the target line will not put you in a proper "open" stance. Any adjustments must be made with your upper body too, since that helps to determine the path of your swing and the flight of your shot. If you don't fight it, your body should comply quite nicely.

5

THE FULL SWING

Loading Up and Letting Go

Many people think the golf swing is all about mechanics and attaining certain positions. *Swing* is really the operative word to keep in mind throughout this chapter. I think that swing is all about fluid motion. I love the term "disciplined freedom."

The place to start is right at address. Don't start from a dead standstill. If you stand over the ball for more than a couple of seconds before you begin your swing, you must keep in motion. Whether that means getting your feet set just right or making a little waggle of the club, whatever it is, don't stand stone-still for 10 seconds and then try to draw the club away from the ball. This will create a jerky start. Gentle motion keeps you from becoming tense.

Keeping in Motion

A lot of players begin with a "waggle" or a forward press, with the right knee moving just toward the target. I like to have the club and my feet in motion a bit. I will use a little forward press with my right knee coming in to kick-start the backswing. It can get your weight moving away from the ball more freely. Jack Nicklaus cocks his head to the right. Tom Kite increases his knee flex just before taking the club away from the ball. Nancy Lopez raises her hands slightly, a move uniquely hers. It's your choice; experiment and see what works for you.

To begin the backswing, start everything together in one piece. The shoulders, arms, hands, and the clubhead all start together as your body turns away from the ball. This is what we mean by a one-piece takeaway. The clubhead sweeps straight away from the ball for a few inches in a good start.

31-time LPGA Tour winner and member of LPGA Hall of Fame

"This got me thinking of my mom and what she does. Too many women lift the club away from the ball rather than sweeping it away with an extended left arm. By lifting, they tend to bend their left arm, which narrows their arc. More width to the takeaway creates more width in the swing. It also helps you to turn and shift your weight to your right side during the backswing."

JUDY'S NOTE: Lifting the club away from the ball is a function of your hands, wrists, and elbows. It is the direct opposite of the desired one-piece takeaway and produces very weak shots.

Takeaway

A one-piece takeaway is the beginning step in developing good timing. The word *timing* is used a lot in discussing the golf swing. I'm not sure that in the first half of my golf life I even knew what that meant, beyond knowing there were days when my timing was off and I just seemed out of sync. I now know there are several moving parts in the swing and a logical sequence of events. Good timing results when the sequence of events is in the proper order.

When everything starts together, you can create a nice comfortable extension with your left arm to establish width in your swing arc. This is very important for women. Since many of us are 5′6″ and under, it's especially important to create an arc that will eventually build clubhead speed. To achieve this, you need a comfortable extension away from the ball. Think of the club as an extension of your left shoulder and your left arm down to the clubhead. Continue that feeling on into the backswing. The importance of a smooth takeaway cannot be overstated.

Wrist Cock

Your wrists begin to cock somewhere about waist-high. Because of the length and weight of the club, your hands instinctively feel a need to help. They will begin to cock. There is a school of thought that this should consciously happen earlier in the swing. I don't recommend this, particularly for those of us who aren't very strong or powerful.

It is important that your hands cock in the right manner. You cock at your wrists just above the left thumb joint. Women tend to have trouble finding the correct and comfortable cocking position. Some can't support the club with their hands and wrists, and it falls too far behind their bodies. This is as important for longtime players as it is for beginners. What I call a "modified tray" position can be seen clearly in the pictures on page 40. This refers to the right-hand position at the top, almost as if you were a waiter carrying a tray.

One-Handed Swing

A strong grip helps achieve the good position we're talking about. You can demonstrate this to yourself with a little experiment. Take a club and put it in your left hand with a weak grip: your left hand turned to the left, with the

THE TAKEAWAY: THE RIGHT AND WRONG WAY TO START. *From a static position (1), many golfers need some kind of waggle or forward press with the right knee to start the club in motion. The swing should begin with the shoulders, arms, hands, and clubhead all starting back together as the body begins to turn.*

As you get to about waist-high, the wrists begin to cock and the toe of the club should be pointing straight up (2).

If you try to keep the clubface too square to the target, the clubface will get closed. It's hard to get the ball airborne from this position (3).

THE "MODIFIED TRAY." *Being able to support the club at the top of the backswing is a big issue for women. If you don't, the club tends to fall back behind your body. The image I was taught is of a "tray" position at the top. It's as if you were a waiter carrying a tray. I demonstrate what I mean here with my right hand open (1) and then closed as it is swinging the club (2). I refer to this position as a "modified tray" because the hand is not completely bent back at the wrist as it would be if you were carrying a heavy tray weighted down with dinner plates.*

PETER ALLISS

BBC and ABC commentator

"If you're wearing a wristwatch, at the top of your backswing, you should be able to tell the time."

JUDY'S NOTE: We talked about how women can't support the club well at the top. If your left wrist is in the correct position at the top of your backswing, the face of your watch should be easy to see. If it's difficult, you've swung the club back in some kind of awkward manner.

1

2

thumb right on top of the grip. Now swing the club back one-handed with that grip while trying to keep your left arm extended. You'll find it very difficult, if you can do it at all. Now put your left hand on the club with your left thumb to the right side of the shaft, the "V" formed by your thumb and forefinger pointing to your right shoulder. Now swing it back and keep your left arm extended. You'll find it's ten times easier. This gives you a real feeling of how you should put your hands on the club and how that helps you to get your swing started properly.

If I could get every beginner to swing the club back with a comfortable extension of the left arm, there would be very few whiffs. Your left arm should be the one constant element of the swing going back and then returning back to the ball.

A STRONG GRIP HELPS TO CREATE EXTENSION. *A one-handed experiment demonstrates one of the inherent benefits of a stronger left-hand grip. Take a club and swing it back with your left arm only. If you have an orthodox grip, you'll find it's hard to keep the*

left arm extended with a one-arm swing (1).

With a stronger grip like mine, the left arm becomes much stronger and left-arm extension becomes much easier right away (2).

Weight Shift

As your backswing begins to gather momentum, it is very important that the bulk of your body weight moves onto your right side. A good backswing is not a lift or slide, but a full, gradual turn away from the ball. In most cases, a full backswing may necessitate raising your left heel to some extent. It

THE RELEASE OF THE LEFT HEEL. *To turn your body during the backswing, you usually need to release your left heel. If the heel wants to lift off the ground going back, let it.*

depends on your degree of hip turn and flexibility. If you feel your left heel rising toward the top of the backswing, let it go. You should strive to make as full a shoulder turn as possible without allowing your weight to move past the point of good balance. If your weight goes too far to the outside of your right foot, you'll lose your balance; if your weight stays too much on the inside of your right foot, you will reverse-pivot—your weight will go back to your left.

A full turn should be a good shoulder coil and maybe 50 percent as much hip turn. As a general rule, women, because of our hip and midsection flexibility, tend to be more full-body turners than men. Modern-day golf instruction has taught us that some hip restriction on the backswing creates torque and, in turn, power. Watch Swedish star Helen Alfredsson when you

THE RELEASE OF THE LEFT HEEL (CONTINUED). *If you make a big backswing coil and the left heel doesn't release, you run the danger of the dreaded "reverse pivot": That's where your weight goes back to your left instead of to the right on the backswing, resulting in a loss of power and control.*

From in front of me, you see the left heel releasing even better to facilitate a full turn of the body.

When the left heel is replanted on the ground, it acts as a "trigger" for the downswing and for your weight to shift back to your left side.

Winner of 15 tournaments, including three LPGA majors

"Most women have trouble setting the club in a good position at the top, because they take it away with their hands. A very, very important key for all players that has helped me through the years is a one-piece takeaway. What I mean by that is, I feel as if my shoulders and arms are an extension of the club, and feel a one-piece 'pushing' motion going back for the first three or four feet. This keeps the club low to the ground and gets your swing on plane."

JUDY'S NOTE: Our little muscles, in this case the hands, shouldn't initiate the swing. If they do, you're getting off to a bad start that will be difficult to recover from.

can. She's a great example of this new power position among women pros. Contrast her with a player who learned the game more like I did, Hollis Stacy. We are still more full-body turners, using more of our hips with our shoulders.

Famed tour teacher David Leadbetter has had great success teaching male golfers a big-muscled, upper-body, coil-type golf swing. But he has told me that he's had limited success teaching this swing to women. The big-muscle, tight-torso, arms-very-connected-to-the-upper-body theory would seem to be far less effective for those of us with strength limitations and a different body build. But it is something that many of the game's top players—men and women—have been working on lately.

When we talk about the big muscles, we mean the legs, shoulders, and torso of the upper body. The small muscles are our hands, wrists, fingers, and forearms. I believe that if your big muscles do the right things, the little muscles will respond appropriately. If the big muscles make the incorrect moves—or don't move at all—then the little muscles try to take over. This almost always ensures failure.

Approaching the Top

As your backswing approaches the top, the majority of your weight is settled solidly on the right heel. The right knee remains slightly flexed. This is very important.

In the process, your upper body may move ever so slightly away from the center. This is all right and is even good. You should not hold your head so still over the ball that you reverse-pivot, with your weight moving left before you complete your backswing. You cannot be a good, consistent golfer if you reverse-pivot. *It is one of the game's absolutes*—and one of the most common errors.

One of the more important factors in developing good timing and nice rhythm is your ability to swing the club to the top. I can't tell you what the top is for you. It is different for each of us. But there is a place in our golf swing, at the top of the backswing, where we are what we call "set." The mechanical facts are that when you get to the top, either you have to stop imperceptibly to change directions, or the club has to change paths. One or the other has to happen for us to go the other way into the downswing. You will do one or the other without making a conscious effort.

I also cannot tell everybody who reads this book how far back you should swing. Parallel should be the ideal for length of swing, meaning the clubhead

AT THE TOP OF BACKSWING. *Getting the club correctly positioned at the top of the backswing is more than half the battle. Here I've got it in a good position, with the hands nicely supporting the club, which is parallel to the target line. This is the desired position, especially for a flatter swinger like me who swings more "around" the body.*

WRONG: *This is what we call "laid off," where the club gets way outside the hands, pointing to the right.*

is pointing more or less on a line parallel to the target line and is parallel to the ground. Parallel, or just short of it, gives you the most control—of the club and your shots. With a driver, the swing will appear to be a bit longer and past parallel, across the target line, because of the length of the shaft. That is something you are going to have to consider. People who make a great big shoulder turn are going to swing the club longer. You can stand in your living room and figure out pretty quickly that, if you can coil your shoulders far enough, the club will cross the line. And some great players have done it, including Bobby Jones, Fred Couples, and Nancy Lopez. If you cross the line because of a big shoulder turn, it is not a problem. If you cross the line because it is something funny that you are doing with your hands and arms, it is a problem. Laura Davies has what I consider just about

SWING UP AND BEHIND YOUR HEAD, NOT OVER IT. *Also wrong: An example of lifting the club up over your right ear (1). When we talk about more-upright swings, we mean that the club should be swung up behind your head, not over it like this.*

Captured here in motion (2), I'm at the top of the backswing with a driver. Note how the hands are supporting the club and the shaft is flexing as the club changes direction. I love this shot!

the ideal backswing length. She does not quite get to parallel. But she does have a huge shoulder turn, and that's where she generates her power—in addition to the fact that she is a tall, strong young woman.

Swing Plane

The plane of the backswing is its imaginary arc. To understand the term, hold a club straight out in front of you, as if it were a baseball bat striking the ball right over home plate. If you created a swing from here, it would be the flattest possible plane. As we bend over in a golf swing and put the club at rest on the ground, each successive angle change makes the swing go from flat to eventually upright. I have a flat plane.

There are a lot of things that dictate what the plane should be for a particular player. In my case I play with a 44-inch driver, which is a long standard for men. When you couple 5'4" height with long arms, a long golf club, and a strong grip, the golf swing cannot be anything other than pretty round and flat. If you have short golf clubs and short arms, obviously you are going to be a lot closer to the ball, and you'll swing the club in a steeper fashion than I do. A strong grip also encourages a flatter swing plane. My hands at the top are very close to the level of my right shoulder. Swinging on a fairly flat plane will naturally bring your hands more inside the line starting down, allowing you to swing the clubhead out toward the target more easily. A more upright plane would have your hands higher than shoulder level. Look for this position when you watch Betsy King.

Taller people and those with weaker grips tend to swing more upright, but among women, this would be the minority. I hate to see anybody lift the club. I like to see one continuous, circular motion, whether flatter or more upright.

One thing I tell people when I teach is, whether your swing is flat, upright, or somewhere in the middle, the important thing is that you swing the club behind your head, *not* over your head. What a lot of people do, watching golf on television and trying to imitate somebody with a pretty upright swing, is to lift the club up and swing the club over their right ear and over their heads. That is not the way to achieve an upright golf swing. Jack Nicklaus is an example. So is rising LPGA player Kelly Robbins. She sets the club high but *behind* her; it is not lifted to get upright.

Trigger at the Top

Now that all this weight has been "loaded up" on your right side, the trigger for changing directions is for that weight to start back to the left. It should not be a quick or violent move. It should be a smooth move, in fact, with the start of your weight returning to your left side. Replanting the weight on the left foot begins this shift, and initiates the driving action of your legs so important to creating distance. Your knees will naturally move toward the left laterally. Let me dispel instruction of a few years ago that had many players thinking they had to slide toward the target through impact. In fact, *as your weight begins to hit your left foot, your left hip will want to start turning out of the way. Let it.* Hence the term you hear often on television, "clearing the left side."

FROM THE TOP, THREE KEY MOVES.

Starting from the top, here's another good shot of me turning behind the ball, supporting the club, and storing up power for the downswing (1). On the return to the ball, my weight begins to transfer to my left side (2) and my hips begin to turn out of the way. Notice that the hands

have delayed their release until impact. After the ball is gone and the club has swung through it, my head has just started to release (3). I've stayed in my posture through impact. A good finishing thought (4) is to finish in balance on your left foot, following the flight of the ball.

As I start down, I am not particularly conscious of the upper part of my body. Rather, my thoughts are on hitting the ball flush, then extending the club through the ball toward the target. The path of the downswing more or less takes care of itself if the lower body and hips trigger this start and begin to uncoil. There is one direct route from the top of the swing that the hands will follow naturally if given the chance.

If that trigger doesn't happen and the upper body begins the first move down, you get the shoulders throwing the club outside and across the line. This is called "coming over the top." From that position, you cannot create any kind of centrifugal force. This big circular motion is all designed for the clubhead to generate speed and help us propel the ball. If we break that circle by throwing our upper body out first, all that centrifugal force is gone—and accuracy, too.

Envision yourself as a puppet with strings. You've got a string connecting your left knee to your hands and the grip of the club at the top of the back-swing. If someone tugged on the string to move your left knee back toward the target, your hands, the club, and your shoulders would immediately drop into place and follow through to the target.

Head Movement

"Keep the head still" is one of those hoary sayings golfers hear. I do not totally subscribe to it myself. I am a firm believer that there is no harm at all in the head moving "off the ball" right and then back to the left. If your head moves up and down, however, you will have trouble. That happens to be one of the faults that I have had over the years when I'm playing poorly. My head will tend to go down a bit on the backswing, which causes me to spring up at the ball and can result in a lot of "thin" shots. A good adage to remember is that successful players always move *toward* the golf ball, while bad players fall away from it. So you always want to have yourself in a position where you *can go to it and through it*.

Curtis Strange made an astute observation to Bob Rosburg in Palm Springs about 15 years ago. He said the object is not to stay behind the ball. The object is to *get* behind the ball so you can move through it.

I see many women who remain too still rather than move too much. This is because they've been told to keep their head still throughout the swing. You cannot hope to be a good player if you hold your head so still over the ball that you reverse-pivot. Many women players would be well served by freeing their head up a little and becoming more in control of their legs

DIVOTS—THE GOOD, THE BAD, AND THE UGLY. *A telltale sign of how you've hit the ball off the fairway is the divots you leave behind. Deep, dug-out divots (left) indicate you've hit the ball from the top.*

What you want are shallow "nipped" divots (right), indicating you've made clean, crisp contact, swinging on the target line. At some courses and driving ranges, these are an endangered species.

and hips on the backswing. For your weight to be in good balance on your right side at the top, you need a slight movement of your upper body. I have seen players who can acheive this while keeping their head quite still, but it is difficult. I think you are better off with a little freedom of movement in your upper body to ensure that you get your right side fully "loaded."

"Moving off the ball"

If you do move "off the ball" slightly, you will be in pretty good company. In my day, there were any number of Japanese players who came to the LPGA Tour. One you may recall was Chako Higuchi. She epitomized "moving off the ball." She would move way off the ball to the right on her backswing and then back through it on the downswing, and she was a very fine player. Because they are so small, I think a lot of Japanese women were taught to move off the ball in an effort to generate some clubhead speed and power.

Letting It Go

When you reach the moment of truth—impact—you should be very conscious of letting everything go, not trying to restrain any of the natural club-head speed that has been developed. This is a perfect example of our bigger muscles creating a good swing path and our little muscles responding. Do not try to control the club at impact. A common flaw is the effort to hold the club*face* square through impact. I see amateur players make this mistake, restricting the extension of the arms and the clubhead by pulling their hands in toward their body—a case of little muscles taking over. You end up cutting across the ball and hitting a weak slice.

With a stronger grip, the clubhead is moving toward the target for a greater length of time. With any grip, a good swing path encourages a good clubface angle. A strong left-hand grip will have you turn the club over through the swing a little later than an orthodox left-hand grip will. This is a natural reaction, though, not a forced one. The swing path is something you have some control over; the direction of the clubface at impact is a reaction to that path.

As you move through the hitting area, feel as if the palm of your right hand represents the clubface. Your head is behind the ball at impact and your hands and arms extend toward the target, because you have let the clubhead go. It's the result of the power you've built up being released.

Early in my career, I was taught to swing the club out to the right after impact. I don't think the club actually goes to the right after the ball has been struck, but the feeling that you are extending it past the impact area promotes a good swing path. Your left arm will fold after impact, about waist-high, but that should happen naturally. You don't have to force it. The right arm, which was bent on the backswing, will be the one that extends on the follow-through. Your arms in the through-swing are a mirror image of your arms in the backswing.

Speed is *generated* in the golf swing. It doesn't happen early or all of a sudden. The term "release" refers to the unleashing of all the power and energy that has been built up by the backswing coil and natural cocking of the wrists. A few feet beyond impact, your upper body has turned away from the line of flight and the club goes on to a finish. You don't actually swing it into a desired finish or follow-through position. I was and am a high finisher, but it occurs as a natural result of my arms swinging out and my left arm folding.

It's important that you maintain your posture through impact. But don't confuse that with "keeping your head down." *It's natural and correct for your head to release and for your eyes to follow the flight of the golf ball.* But you must guard against the action of pulling out of your posture earlier than necessary.

A final thought: It's good practice to complete your swing in balance, with your weight on your left foot, following the flight of the ball.

It's One Swing

As the club gets longer, your stance gets wider and the ball position moves more forward as you are standing farther away from it. This, more than anything, accounts for the difference in your swing with different clubs. I don't

LONGER CLUB EQUALS LONGER SWING. *I'm making the same swing but with two different clubs. With a driver (right), the swing will appear longer because the club is longer. "Parallel," like this, is the preferred position—you do not want to swing much past this point.*

believe you consciously need to do anything different in your swing motion. The swing with the driver tends to be longer and more sweeping, because the ball is teed. Swings with the shorter irons will be steeper and shorter, because of your club's lie and length, and the ball's position, creating more of a descending action. You should not be afraid to swing *through the turf*. That's the sign of a good player: shallow, nipped divots. That's what you'll see on the practice tee at any tour stop. Far too many women are afraid of taking divots. Don't be.

With the driver, you need to tee the ball up a decent height. The general rule has been that half of the ball should be visible above the top edge of the clubface. Now, with many of the big-headed drivers that help to get the ball into the air, that is changing somewhat. We used to tee it much higher with wooden clubs. It's really a matter of experimenting with what works best for you, depending on what kind of driver you're using. Anytime you have a chance to use a tee—on a par-3 hole with an iron, for example—do it. Why not give yourself a perfect lie?

SWING SEQUENCE WITH THE DRIVER FROM FACE-ON. *(1) Ball positioned off left toe.*

(2) Low, sweeping takeaway. (3) Extension and turn. (4) Creating a wide arc on the way back.

SWING SEQUENCE WITH THE DRIVER FROM FACE-ON (CONTINUED). *(5) Halfway into the backswing. (6) Just beginning to change directions, weight starting back to left side. (7) Hands storing power for impact. (8) Hands have released and turned over. (9 and 10) Swinging into a high finish.*

SWING SEQUENCE WITH THE DRIVER FROM DOWN THE LINE. *(1) Address. (2) Start of the takeaway, with club going straight away from the ball for a short distance. (3) Wide arc from the left* shoulder. *(4) Turning to get behind the ball. (5) Starting to change directions. (6) Swinging from the inside. (7) Swinging through to a high finish. (8) Finishing in balance on the left foot.*

SWING SEQUENCE WITH AN IRON.
(1) Ball still positioned forward of center. (2) One-piece takeaway. (3) Good clubface position, almost waist-high. (4) Hands begin to break about waist-high. (5) Near top of backswing. (6)Weight starts back to left side—uncoiling begins. (7) Coming from the inside to impact. (8) Hips turn through, hands begin to release.

SWING SEQUENCE WITH AN IRON
(CONTINUED). *(9) Hands released, club swinging*
to target. (10) Hands turning over. (11) Balanced finish.

Tempo and Timing

If you're a person who tends to do things quickly, who's always on the run, who walks and talks fast, chances are that's how you'll swing the golf club. If you are a deliberate, slow mover and talker, your swing may also tend to be slower. The key to a successful tempo is one that feels natural and is easy to repeat. I see more people who swing too fast rather than too slow, especially when they are under pressure. I also see a lot of people who start out nice and slow and then get herky-jerky when they get to the top of their backswing. When I find myself getting too quick, I return to the simple thought of extending the club away with my left side, and it makes me slow down automatically. By concentrating on extension, I make my arc a bit bigger and my turn fuller, and the whole action takes a bit more time to complete.

Whatever your tempo—slow, fast, or somewhere in between—the secret is to make it the same, day in and day out. This will take some of the variables out of your game. Consistent tempo brings on consistent timing, and can help to camouflage some mistakes in your swing. Nancy Lopez's greatest swing attribute is her ability to maintain exactly the same tempo whether playing golf with her daughters or trying to win a championship.

Ernie Els, the 1994 U.S. Open champion, stands out for another reason. At 6'3" and 210 pounds, he exemplifies smoothness and tempo. My son, who is just as tall and very strong, observed that no big man has ever impressed him more with his smoothness than Els. In contrast, other big men such as John Daly and Mark Calcavecchia leave no question that they are trying to be powerful. Els shows that you don't have to swing fast and hard to create clubhead speed. He has opted for smoothness and tempo to generate tremendous power.

Repetition is really the key to a good, solid golf swing. You need to find something that you can do reasonably well and repeat it over and over. Lee Trevino is probably the greatest repeater the game has ever seen. There are so many good things about his swing. He sets up open and keeps the club on line probably longer than any player I've seen, and his ball-striking with that patented fade has been remarkably consistent. As a result, he's had very few real "down" times in his career aside from when he's been injured. His bad days have been pretty good.

When you find a swing that lets you hit the ball best, repeat it—and bottle it!

10 More Yards: The Never-Ending Quest

Distance is an issue for women players at all levels. Even tour pros continually search for an extra 10 yards. We're always looking for something to help us hit it farther. My own suggestions have been pretty well set forth throughout this book. To reiterate, I'd say the best things you can do are to strengthen your grip and try a longer driver. But I don't claim to have a corner on the market as far as expertise. So I asked some other people, friends I work with and know from the tours, what one tip they would give women who are looking for that elusive 10 more yards. Here's what they had to say.

CAUTION: DON'T TRY ALL OF THESE AT ONCE. Read through them; surely one or two will apply to you. I've added my own comments to help you better understand each tip. A couple of them may seem slightly contradictory, but they actually aren't. For example, you can have great rhythm and still be aggressive.

HELEN ALFREDSSON

Six-time Swedish national champion

"We were always taught to swing slow with a good tempo. But you have to have some acceleration throughout the swing. I think that's where a lot of women go wrong. They should just try to whack it a few times and see what happens."

JUDY'S NOTE: Speed needs to be generated. Starting slow does not mean swinging slow. *Acceleration* is the operative word here.

BETH DANIEL

32-time LPGA Tour winner, including the 1990 LPGA Championship

"I'd tell everyone, not just women, to work on their rhythm. If you watch a tour player or a good amateur player try to hit the ball longer, they don't swing faster or harder at it—they make a fuller, more fluid golf swing. And I think that's what you have to work on in order to get more clubhead speed."

JUDY'S NOTE: The best players call up their best shots with their best swings, not their hardest, fastest efforts.

MARLENE HAGGE

Charter member of LPGA and 25-time Tour winner

"I feel very strongly that women don't do what men do to create power. Women don't know how to use their legs. They aren't used to using their legs in the same way men do. If you just watch a woman stand, she's not using her legs to stand with. She's leaning on her legs, always resting on her legs, rather than using the leg muscles and the strength in her legs. Women have to set up with a stronger foundation and learn to build power from the lower half of their bodies."

JUDY'S NOTE: To fully understand the importance of your lower body, imagine yourself suspended off the ground, without any traction, trying to create power with a swing. After playing golf years ago with Bob Toski and Hall of Fame hitter Ted Williams, I sat in on an afternoon-long discussion between these two experts about power. Ted believed his power source was his very powerful arms and shoulders. Bob insisted that without the traction from his feet and stepping into the pitch with his leg, his power would be much less. I agreed with Toski, and I'm not sure Ted didn't in the end.

TOM KITE

19-time winner on tour, including the 1992 U.S. Open

"The best players in the world today are working on building resistance with their lower body against the coil of the upper body. I see a lot of women who swing a golf club with their hip joints being too loose. As a result, they over-turn with their lower bodies, the legs becoming somewhat useless, and they don't store and build power."

JUDY'S NOTE: Tom is saying that if you're going to work on coiling more, it should be in your shoulders and in the upper portion of your body, not with your legs and hips. Over-turning there creates a power-robbing reverse pivot.

SANDRA POST

1979 Colgate Dinah Shore champion and TV commentator

"A lot of women misunderstand the role of the legs in the golf swing. By overusing them on the backswing, they actually break down. Their left knee will go over and actually 'kiss' the right knee. When they do that they get very wobbly, and they'll hit behind the ball and hit it very inconsistently. I tell my students to imagine there's a soccer ball between their knees. If you do that, your legs will stay firmer and stronger and you'll hit the ball much more consistently."

JUDY'S NOTE: If you actually did the soccer-ball drill, you would stay tall through the backswing and avoid any inclination to reverse-pivot.

DAVIS LOVE III

Nine-time PGA Tour winner, including 1992 Players Championship

"I remember my dad telling my mom not to *try* to hit it any farther. There was only so far that she was going to hit it, so she shouldn't try to force the ball to go very far. When she got quick and tried to hit it hard, she'd mis-hit it, and the ball really didn't go anywhere. But when she made a good full turn and would swing the club, she'd hit it as far as she could. So, I just always remember him preaching rhythm to her, and a nice smooth swing."

JUDY'S NOTE: Excuse the violent terms: If I draw back and punch you, trying to use only my muscular strength, I probably won't hurt you. But when I draw my hand back, cocking my wrist, and I let that hand go, I've created more speed than I can with a punch, and the force of the blow could sting. In one, I've tried to use my strength to create power; in the other, I have wound up and let go.

STEVE MELNYK

ABC golf commentator and 1969 U.S. Amateur champion

"Distance is not always a question of strength, particularly for women. It's a question of speed. If a woman can learn to swing the club faster, she'll hit the ball farther. You do so with a light grip pressure, as well as a proper setup. But I've had a lot of success with women who were convinced they couldn't hit it very far, but once they were determined to step up there and swing the club fast, they picked up considerable distance."

JUDY'S NOTE: Our tendency as women is to be somewhat nonaggressive. It helps to adopt a more aggressive approach to the golf swing . . . and the game itself. The light grip Steve recommends helps to translate swinging faster into clubhead speed. It allows you to let the club go and not try to force it to go, one of my continuing themes.

LOUISE SUGGS

Charter member of LPGA Tour and 50-time Tour winner

"I think it's difficult for women to release the club and let it turn over. They've seen so many stop-action pictures that start at address and return to impact with the club still square. They see that and have misconstrued it to think the club is supposed to *stay* square through the impact area, instead of letting it release and turn over."

JUDY'S NOTE: I wanted to include Louise to provide contrast to this dead-hands, torso-driven, big-muscle theory of today. She was such a great hands player, with a wonderful sense of rhythm and tempo. She was always letting her hands work for her. She created clubhead speed the old-fashioned way, just by kind of swinging the clubhead. She was a beautiful ball-striker, wonderfully consistent. Today, in her 70s, she still hits it beautifully. This is someone who is not very tall and is of average physical strength at best. And yet she created clubhead speed without a lot of effort. There's no reason a lot of women can't do this.

LAURA DAVIES

11-time LPGA Tour winner, including the 1987 U.S. Women's Open

"You have to learn to hit a draw. Aim the clubface where you want the ball to finish—let's say down the middle. Then close your feet, hips, and shoulders. They should be aiming down the right side of the fairway.

"With your normal swing, this combination will impart right-to-left spin. You should be able to hit a draw and be fairly accurate as well."

JUDY'S NOTE: A right-to-left shot can be produced only with the club swinging slightly from the inside to the impact area and toward the target. Laura's tip encourages that swing path.

JAN STEPHENSON

16-time LPGA Tour winner, including the 1983 U.S. Women's Open

"I hate to say this, but I think they should try to copy the new men's swings, which means using the big muscles. I see so many women amateurs who are still making the old reverse weight shift with the lower body. I've gained distance by trying to restrict my hip turn and coil more with my upper body. I feel like I almost have no backswing compared to the old days, because I'm trying to get more torque. But someone like me, as weak as I am, I'm going to lose flexibility as I get older, so I felt like I needed to do it.

"If I were starting all over again, I'd lift weights and try to become tighter and stronger. It's a power game today."

JUDY'S NOTE: An upper-body and shoulder turn, coupled with a restricted hip and lower-body turn, stores energy. Do a similar thing with a rubber band, rotating the upper part and holding the lower end still; and when you let go, it releases energy. If I turn the entire rubber band at the same time, there isn't any energy stored.

JULI INKSTER

15-time Tour winner and three-time U.S. Amateur champion

"I recommend a compact swing. The looser you get, the more distance you lose. You know, take it up there and pause a little bit at the top. Then come back down so you get your timing going, and I think you'll gain more yards. I know that when my timing's the best, I hit the ball farther."

JUDY'S NOTE: Overswinging—swinging your arms and the club past the point you are able to turn—does not produce power.

CURTIS STRANGE

17-time PGA Tour winner, including 1988 and 1989 U.S. Open

"Women need to hit hooks, turning the ball from right to left off the tee for maximum distance. A little extra loft helps you to do that. Sometimes, it's even worthwhile to drive off the tee with a 3-wood."

JUDY'S NOTE: From your woods through the long irons, the straighter the face of the club—those with the least loft—the harder it is to turn the ball over with right-to-left spin. Taken to the extreme, though—when you get down to a 9-iron and your wedges—those clubs with the most loft are the most difficult to curve.

HALE IRWIN

20-time PGA Tour winner, including three U.S. Opens

"What I see is, most women, by their body build, do not turn their shoulders as well as they could. They tend to sway from side to side, rather than turning their hips. Consequently they become very up-right, swinging their arms up and down rather than around their bodies. My suggestion would be to concentrate on turning the shoulders and letting the arms follow."

JUDY'S NOTE: As your posture improves, turning and not swaying will become easier. When you turn away more freely, you'll be less apt to swing your arms up and down.

DOTTIE PEPPER

Winner of 10 LPGA Tour events, including 1992 Nabisco Dinah Shore

"I think women tend to ignore the lower half of their bodies. They think because their arms are connected to that golf club, that's where their power comes from. They don't start the swing from the top, with the bottom. They tend to be very handsy. If they could learn to initiate their downswing with the lower body, I think that would make a big difference in terms of power."

JUDY'S NOTE: Using your lower body as a trigger to change directions for the downswing helps you to store power for impact. You've turned and shifted your weight to the right; this is the time that it begins smoothly moving back to the left.

6

PUTTING

The Stroke, the Speed, and the Read

Women golfers, even professionals, have never been as good at putting as we could be. That was an observation made by many of the players I interviewed for this book. Although there are many more good putters on the LPGA Tour now than when I played, a disparity still exists between men and women when we get on the greens. Because strength is absolutely not a factor, I see no reason why women can't putt as well as men. I hope to give you some thoughts and tips in this chapter that will help you bridge this gap.

In 1995 the big trend on tour was toward a cross-handed putting method, with the left hand below the right. It's considered slightly unorthodox, but it is an excellent way to putt, especially because it stabilizes the left wrist, which often breaks down at impact. The use of this method by so many respected, top players—Fred Couples, Paul Azinger, Nick Faldo, Tom Kite, Jan Stephenson, Beth Daniel, and 1995 LPGA champion Kelly Robbins—was similar in some ways to the newfound respect and popularity of the "strong" full-swing grip. And it reconfirmed an old truism about golf: It isn't how, but how many. However you can get it in the hole with the fewest strokes is the best method for you.

I personally use a reverse overlap grip: My two thumbs are basically along the top of the grip. The forefinger of my left hand then goes over the last three fingers of my right hand. It gives me more of the feeling of my two hands working as one. That's really the ultimate goal with any grip—not to feel like one hand is doing one task and the other another. There are other variations that are covered in the photos accompanying this chapter. But the two hands feeling like one is the common denominator that we all seek.

TOM KITE

Winner of more than $9 million on PGA Tour

"As a general rule, most women I have seen are pitiful putters. They can all be better if they just work at it. But they have to spend some time working at it. The lack of practice is a big reason they're poor putters."

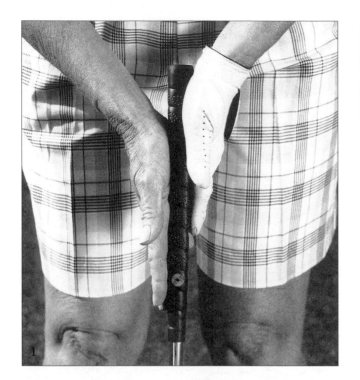

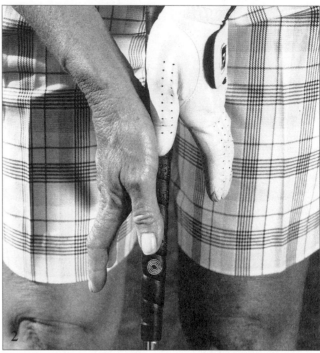

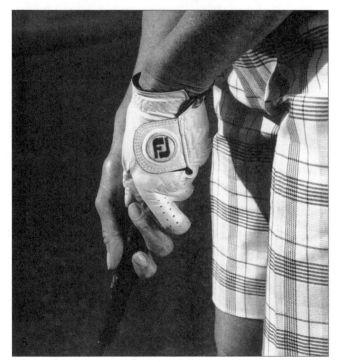

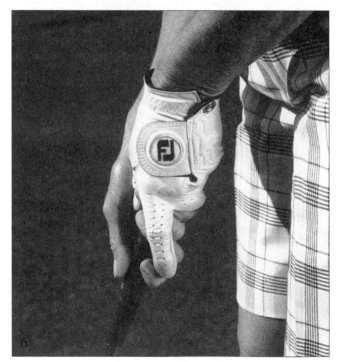

A VARIETY OF GRIPS TO CHOOSE FROM.

Whatever putting grip you use, the overriding goal is to have the two palms facing each other and working together (1 and 2).

In the conventional overlap grip (3), the last three

fingers of the left hand wrap underneath and meet the thumb, with the right pinkie overlapping between the middle finger and forefinger of the right hand.

The reverse overlap grip (4–6) is the one I use. The forefinger of my left hand goes over the last three fingers of

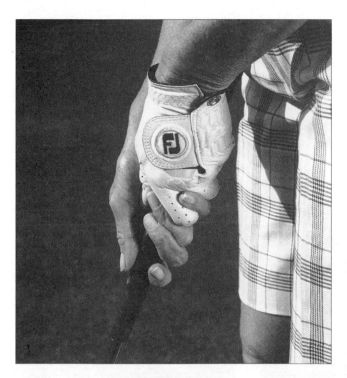

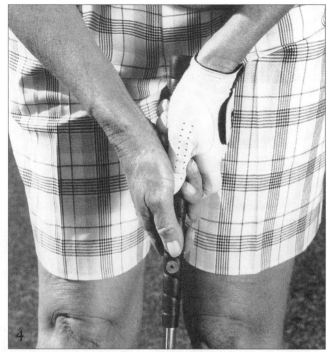

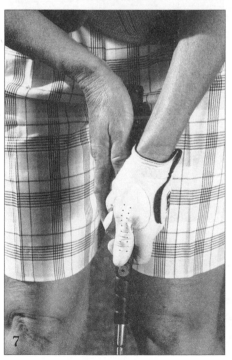

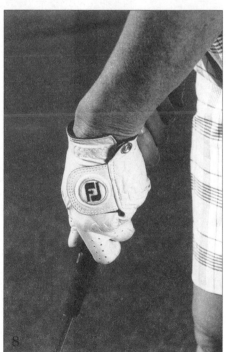

my right hand, giving me even more of a feeling of the two hands working together.

The cross-handed grip (7–9) reverses the hands, putting the left hand below the right. This helps to square the shoulders and stabilize the left wrist. In recent years, some of the top players on tour have gone to this grip, once considered a last-ditch effort for those who had lost their touch on the greens.

Setup

I position the ball somewhat forward in my stance, off my left heel. That, like much of putting, is largely a matter of personal preference. If you play the ball a little more forward, you have to be sure to keep your hands forward, too. At worst, you want the putter shaft straight up and down, but the best position to create nice, true overspin is to have the hands ever so slightly ahead of the ball. Getting your hands behind the ball usually promotes a poor touch, and speed control is the ultimate key to putting. Having

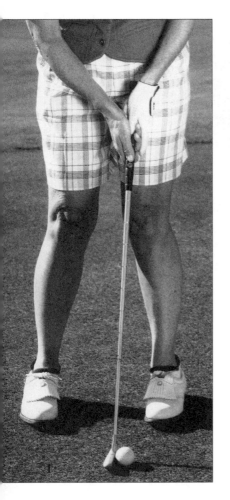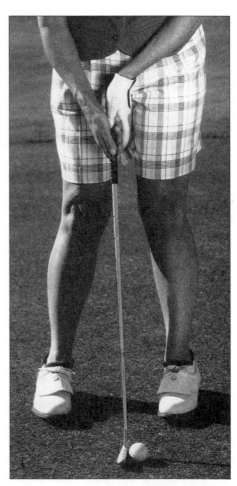

BALL AND HAND POSITIONING. *As you line up to putt, the ball should be positioned just inside your left foot and your hands should fall slightly ahead of the ball (1).*

Your hands should be even with the ball and the shaft should be more or less straight up and down (2).

When you get your hands behind the ball (3), you are going to have problems with speed.

the hands behind the ball is especially bad on longer putts, because you just cannot get the ball rolling true enough.

Keep your eyes over the ball

You need to have your eyes over the ball, because that's the best way to see the line and enhance your ability to keep the putterhead more or less straight back and through. The best way to accomplish this is to stand with your knees slightly flexed and do your bending at your hip joints and—unlike for the full swing—slightly at your waist. You have to bend in the midsection to get your eyes over the line of the putt. If there is any leeway, your eyes

MAKE SURE YOUR EYES ARE OVER THE BALL. *By dropping the putter below your eye line, you can check to make sure your eyes are directly over the ball (1). If you must err here, it should be to the inside of the ball.*

In these photos I've got it too far inside (2) and then too far out over the ball (3). Once you get that far outside, you're not going to make many putts.

could be slightly inside the line. But you should never bend so far as to put your eyes on the outside of the line. You cannot putt from that position.

You also need good balance. It's best to get your weight distributed evenly, never just on your toes or on your heels. The tendency is to get your weight too far toward your toes. That is a tension creator. When you are all set, see if you can wiggle your toes. You should feel that you are in a slight sitting position with your muscles relaxed. This allows you to sense and feel and develop a touch.

The Stroke

The predominant school of thought these days says take the hands out of the stroke—use the arms and shoulders to swing like a pendulum, with "dead"

AN ALL-HANDS STROKE LEADS TO A WRIST BREAKDOWN. *The putting stroke should be a combination of an arm swing and some hand and* *wrist motion. When you try to do it all with your hands (right), the left wrist breaks down and you start "flipping" at the ball, not stroking it.*

hands (meaning quiet wrists). Many fine putters do this, but I'm not sure it's for everyone, especially infrequent or beginning golfers. There have also been some very successful putters—Nancy Lopez and Gary Player, to name two—who have used more of a handsy, "pop" stroke with great effectiveness.

In the later years of my playing career and now, I've putted with what I call a "combination" stroke. My arms swing from my shoulders, but I combine it with a little movement in my hands and wrists. I believe my arm stroke provides consistency, while my hands and small amount of wrist movement provide touch and feel. I think this method is particularly good for people who don't play golf every day.

However, no matter what style you use, you want to stay reasonably still in the upper body as you stroke the ball. Movement is neither necessary nor desirable.

THE COMBINATION STROKE. *Here is my stroke. It's controlled by my arms swinging from my shoulders. While you don't want too much hand action, I don't believe in totally eliminating hands from the stroke,* *either, especially if you don't play golf every day. The arms swinging provide the consistency. The hands and a small amount of wrist movement provide the touch-and-feel part.*

The combination stroke (continued).

You hear a lot about keeping the blade "square." The putter should travel more or less back and through along an extension of the target line. As the stroke gets a little longer, the blade will naturally come inside that line. You can work too hard at keeping your stroke perfectly square and "on line," and I think it needs to be more natural than that.

One of the keys to good putting is learning what length stroke allows you to putt the ball a certain distance. This may be where men have had an advantage; due to their backgrounds in other sports, they seem to have an instinctive feel for what it takes. You can develop a feel by just rolling a ball underhanded across a putting green. From 20 feet, roll it to the hole. You shouldn't think about how far back to swing your arm to make the ball go the right distance. And you shouldn't have conscious thoughts about how far back to take the putter. Let your senses do the work. If you don't interfere, your eyes will send a message to your brain, and your hands and arms will react accordingly. In the delicate art of putting, practicing to develop a feel for speed control is paramount.

IT'S AS EASY AS . . . ROLLING A BALL. *In putting, you need to develop a sixth sense for the length of stroke needed to get the ball to roll the right distance. By pitching a ball underhanded and rolling it toward the cup, you instinctively feel how far back your arm has to swing to make the ball go the right distance.*

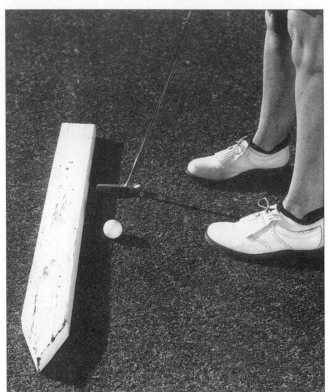

THE BOARD DRILL. *Putting against a directional board illustrates how the stroke must accommodate the length of the putt. On a shorter putt, the putter can and does stay pretty much straight back and through on the line to the hole. But as the stroke gets longer (bottom photo), the putter necessarily has to come inside the target line.*

THE FLAT SPOT.

There is an area several inches behind the ball that I call the "flat area" for putting. Here, and just in front of the ball after impact, the putter remains low to the ground. On this particular putt, a four-footer, I'm at the completion of my backstroke, and you can see that the putter has barely left the turf.

NANCY LOPEZ

45 career victories and member of LPGA Hall of Fame

"I putt from a slightly open stance, with the ball positioned off my left heel. This stance helps me see the line of my putt more easily. My eyes are inside the target line. Unlike some players who 'jab' their putts, I concentrate on making a smooth stroke and accelerating through the ball."

I believe your backswing should be nearly equal to the follow-through. If your stroke is too short, you're going to be forced to "hit" the ball. If your stroke is too long, you're going to have to "quit" on it, or decelerate. Neither of these is desirable. In fact, I became a much better putter later in my career when I developed a more "equal" stroke and quit trying to accelerate so much at impact.

Tom Kite and I had an interesting talk about this in the late 1970s when I was struggling with my putting. In my effort to accelerate through the ball, I became jerky and often hit the ball off line. Tom said that the stroke doesn't have to accelerate through impact, but it *cannot* get slower. I agree. It is absolutely necessary that your putter not lose speed. If it simply maintains its speed through impact, particularly on very good greens, you can be a good putter. However, if you play on poorer, slower greens, accelerating through impact becomes necessary to get the ball rolling at the speed you need. The key in this case is the smoothness of the acceleration.

Nine-time LPGA Tour winner, including 1993 World Championship of Women's Golf

"Women tend to have a poor sense of speed in putting. They need to work in short increments of three or six feet. A lot of people don't know how hard they have to hit a three-footer. They need to go to the putting green each time they go to the golf course and hit a bunch of three- to six-footers to get a feel for how hard they have to hit them."

JUDY'S NOTE: Dottie creates pressure situations for herself while practicing putting. She requires herself to make a series of putts from eight feet and in before she quits. If she misses one along the way, she starts all over again. She is very disciplined. Doing this drill will make you more disciplined, too.

You often hear about how the putter has to stay low to the ground. That's true. There's an area—two or three inches behind the ball and a couple of inches in front of the ball after impact—that I call the "flat area," where you need to keep the putter low. But you don't want to force the putter to stay low as the stroke gets longer. That is awkward and will not produce good results. When you have to swing the putter back farther than three or four inches, it has to come up off the ground somewhat. On the other hand, don't allow your hands to pick the putter straight up. That won't work either.

The best putters seem not to have any extremes in their stroke. What they do is pretty natural for them, and they don't have to force a great deal. This improves their sense of touch and feel. If you are forcing a lot of awkward, unnatural moves, you won't have much feel, and you cannot be a good putter without feel.

Stay still over the ball

An awful lot of putts are missed because of what I call "anxiety attacks." If your head moves, the blade also moves an infinitesimal amount, just enough to miss a short putt. Resist the temptation to look up too soon. Keep your eyes on the ball and where the ball was for just a split second after impact, to make sure anxiety doesn't ruin an otherwise good putt. You can't make any quick or false moves or you are going to affect the direction of your putt. Peter Jacobsen, who worked with ABC in 1993, says this was one thing he noticed from the booth. The pros who missed kept "peeking" at their putts. And since Peter's become more aware of this, he's been playing the best golf of his life.

The yips

If your nerves take over and cause you to twitch and miss short putts, in extreme cases it's called "having the yips." It happens to a lot of people. Beginning at about eight feet, when the hole gets in your peripheral vision, you have a natural urge to want to look at the hole and see where you have putted. The yips rarely happen from 30 feet. It's when you get closer to the hole that it becomes a factor. I believe darting, jumpy eyes are a big cause of the problem. The eye twitch then becomes a hand and body twitch; hence the yips.

A good drill to overcome the yips is to practice putting short putts, listening for the ball to drop. Don't look, just listen. It will build the habit of focusing on the ball, not the hole, and you might start dropping more of

NO HEAD AND BODY MOVEMENT. *There shouldn't be much head and body movement during a putting stroke. Note how my hands and wrists swing back and through, my legs don't move, and my head position stays the same—it doesn't move off the same spot on the pine trees in the background.*

those troubling short putts. *Quiet eyes make for a still head*—and a smoother stroke.

Stand up or bend more?

Again, there are two schools of thought on this, and you have to discover what works best for you. I decided to stand up straighter and become a more upright putter in midcareer, and I believe I putted better under pressure. I found that when I bent over the ball more in my setup, I would get even

MY SIX-STEP ROUTINE FOR CONSISTENT PUTTING. *It helps to do the same thing on each shot in golf, especially with something so precise as putting. My routine is to get between the ball and the hole to see the line and the distance (1); then I get behind the putt (2). I might plumb-bob if I'm not quite sure of the line and need reinforcement (3). Then I take a practice putting stroke to ingrain the right length of stroke (4), put the blade down behind the ball (5), and set my feet in a comfortable position, and I stroke the putt (6). This doesn't have to take very long!*

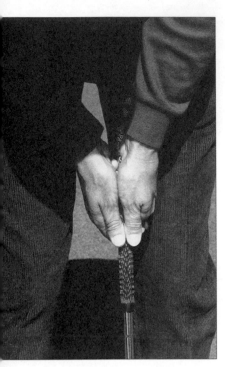

LITTLE'S MAGIC TOUCH. *Sally Little demonstrates her putting grip, with the palms directly facing each other and both thumbs on the shaft. The way her hands worked so well together—and her beautiful tempo—made her a superb putter on fast greens.*

lower under pressure, and I had less and less confidence in short putts. That's certainly not been the case for Jack Nicklaus, but it was for me.

In the 1976 Dinah Shore, I had played one of the finest rounds of my life on Saturday from tee to green but had absolutely mangled it with my putting and shot a 71. I woke up in the middle of the night—I couldn't sleep—and told my husband, Yippy, "Either I am choking to death with the putter or I am getting in my own way and can't move." I went out the next day and decided that no matter what happened, I was going to stand up like a wooden Indian on the putting green. And I did. I have very long arms, so, unlike Ben Crenshaw, who stands up and lets his arms hang freely, I still have some bend in my arms even when I stand up straight. But it didn't take many putts to realize that my arms swung from my shoulders much more easily, and I saw the line in a different way. I won the Dinah Shore that day, shooting 68 in a horrible windstorm and putting very well. From that day on, I have stood tall to the ball.

Routine

Routine is important in putting. The first thing I always do is get my hands on the putter comfortably and set the blade down on the line that I want to start the ball. Then I set my feet down without too much formality. Your feet do not have to be on an exact parallel line to the line of your putt. The only really important consideration is that the blade or the face of the putter is aimed on the intended line.

I suggest a little more casual approach with your setup. I emphasize comfort rather than mechanics. You want a ball position that gets your hands over the ball, even or slightly ahead of the putterhead. After that, I look at the hole once or twice, and I putt. Practice strokes can give you rhythm and/or feel, but should not be overdone; one will do. Notice how Dave Stockton—by all accounts one of the best putters ever—does not take any practice strokes.

Sally and Nancy: Different Strokes

Sally Little for years was one of the best putters on the LPGA Tour. She gripped the putter with both palms directly across from each other. She has a beautifully consistent tempo to her stroke, which helped her to be an excellent fast-green putter. She's shot some phenomenal scores on the fastest greens you can imagine. It always looked like her hands were working together and her wrists were very quiet.

A very different type of putter, with a more wristy action, is Nancy Lopez. In fact, she uses more wrist than almost any other good putter I know today. She takes a little bit more of a "pop" at the ball, and over a long period of time is probably the best female putter I have ever seen. Lopez integrates pop putting with great tempo. That's the key to her style. You'll notice that Lopez's arms and shoulders move very little from the beginning of her stroke. Most of the motion is in her hands. She has been able to keep the tempo of her stroke the same, regardless of the pressure or the situation. This certainly requires a very solid set of nerves!

Over the years, as the competition has gotten keener and the money bigger in golf, people have tried to take the "little muscles" out of their games, especially in putting. They're afraid they won't hold up under the gun. So we've evolved into a sort of dead-hands, arms-swinging-from-the-shoulder type of stroke, born from the need to perform under intense pressure—and because a lot of golf today is played on greens that are finely manicured and very fast.

HARVEY PENICK'S TIP. *In the one lesson I took from the late Texas teacher, he taught me how to take a range ball and line it up with the hole. If you're imparting sidespin to your putts, the stripe will wobble all over the place. Try Harvey's tip if you're lipping out a lot of little putts. It helps to restore solid contact—and confidence!*

APPROACHING ON FOOT GIVES YOU AN INSTINCTIVE FEEL FOR THE BREAK. *One of the pluses of playing golf on foot—walking as opposed to riding in a cart—is that you get an instinctive feel for how the putt is going to break as you approach the front of the green. "First sight is usually right," as they say. When you ride a cart, you usually come into the green from the side and don't have this opportunity to scope out the line.*

This style eliminates some problems, but requires some practice to develop a sense of touch and feel. Tour pros work at this six or seven days a week. That's not the case for the average player, and certainly not the beginner. So I think you need your hands for feel, and the answer might be a kind of combination stroke in which your arms do swing from your shoulders but you also use your hands for a sense of touch and feel. The same holds true in chipping and pitching, as we'll talk about later.

A Penick Pointer

I took one lesson from Harvey Penick, the late, great Texas teacher. He showed me two little drills that worked for me and might help you, too.

The first was to take a range ball on the putting green and put that stripe right on the line with the hole on a reasonably flat putt. Now, if you can putt the ball so that the stripe doesn't wobble, you're hitting the ball pretty solidly and you're not putting any right or left spin on it. If you're

THE LINE-UP DRILL. *To get a feel for breaking putts, line up a series of three or four putts around the hole on a slope from about six feet. Each one will have a*

slightly different break. In these photos, the tee peg just above the cup represents where you want to start the putt. Aim there! Don't push or pull putts to allow for break.

putting sidespin on it, the stripe on the ball will go all goggly-wog. This is a good little drill, especially if you have a lot of putts that are lipping out or look like they're going in and don't. The more solid and true your stroke is, the more true that stripe will roll to the hole.

His second tip was to mark a golf ball with chalk, then set the ball down so the putter will strike the chalk mark. Then you look at your putter and see where the chalk left its mark. This will tell you how close you're hitting the ball to the center, or "sweet spot," of the putter. If it's consistently to one side of center or the other, you can see the correction you need to make.

Green Reading

Green reading is an art, not a science, and much of it is intuitive. The pros on TV go through elaborate rituals, some of which are unnecessary. Obviously, the lay of the land, the slope of the green, and how a ball moves off of that slope are always relative to the speed the ball is rolling. And you must have a certain discipline to roll the ball the right speed for the line you've chosen. Putting is a combination of finding the right line and starting the ball on that line you've chosen at the right speed. Get the line right but mis-hit the putt or hit it the wrong speed, and you'll still miss.

I like to think in terms of the high and low parts of the green. The ball breaks toward the low part. Figuring out which way water drains off the green will indicate where the low part is.

If you walk when you play—as I prefer—one of the best ways to read greens is simply by looking at the lay of the land as you approach the front of the green and go up to mark your ball. You are going to have a sense right there and then as to what the putt is going to do. Ninety percent of the time, your first instinct will be correct. Second-guessing on closer inspection is rarely as accurate as that first impression. All of this working and working on the line is more about getting ready to putt than actually getting added information.

A Closer Look

Most players read putts by standing to the side, halfway between the ball and the hole. I always go to the left side of the line, because my perspective is better. Many players prefer to go to the lower side of the line because they think they can see the break better. In the case of a downhill putt, sometimes it's helpful to get to the other side of the hole (below the break). This is the only time I go to the other side of the hole. For the most part, you'll see everything you need in terms of the break from one side or the other and behind the ball.

You'll often see players who, for more precision, get down to try to see the way the grain is going. Maybe it's for effect, but if it builds your confidence and doesn't slow play too much, I suppose it's OK. Then you see players plumb-bobbing. There is a difference of opinion in the golf community about the value of plumb-bobbing. If it's something that can give you some confidence in the line you're going to choose, it's generally a good tool. Realistically, it's probably not as accurate as some people think it is. From behind the ball—whether standing or crouching—take your putter and hold it in your thumb and forefinger. From those two fingers, let it hang free in front of you. Then, with your dominant eye (in my case, the left), and with the putter hanging free, line the *lower portion* of the shaft of the putter up with your golf ball. Now, looking with your dominant eye, the upper portion of the shaft will fall either right, left, or on the ball. That would be the position on which you want to start your putt—the place where the upper part of the shaft falls will be the "high" side of the hole.

Usually, I think you want to get more general information on the longer putts. You don't need to go through this elaborate, precise procedure for putts of 25 feet or longer. There you need to take a broader view of the line,

WHEN YOU DIAL LONG DISTANCE, SPEED IS PARAMOUNT. *On longer putts, speed becomes more critical than direction. Precision green reading isn't nearly as important on a 40- or 50-footer as having the right distance. All you want with these putts is to get them close—and the better your distance control, the better chance you have of two-putting. If it falls in, great!*

ROLL BALLS TO WITHIN A FOOT OF THE CUP. *A challenging practice drill is to hit putts from long range—say 30-footers—and try to leave them all within a circle around the cup measuring 24 inches in diameter. If you can leave everything within a foot of the hole, you won't have many three-putts.*

because speed is so important on a longer putt. The longer the putt, the more likely we are to misjudge the necessary speed. Obviously, if a putt breaks severely, you have to allow for it, but a great feel for distance will prove to be more important than precise green reading.

Reading Grain

Especially on Bermuda grass that you find in tropical places such as Florida, reading grain becomes a factor. Grain is the direction in which the grass lies

FROM THE FRINGE, STICK WITH YOUR PUTTER. *When your ball is just off the putting surface and in the fringe, or "frog hair," the putter, or "Texas wedge," remains the club you'll get the most consistent results with. By choking up on the putter and gripping it a bit firmer than you normally would, you'll impart the extra oomph you need to get the ball through that grass.*

as it grows, and if it is with you (toward the hole), the putt will be much faster than if it is against you. A general rule of thumb is that the grain will go to the west, to the setting sun. It's not always easy to see, but the grass almost looks like little fingers, and you're trying to tell in which direction they are pointing. A lot of players will say the green looks "shiny" when the grain is with you and dull when it is into you. Another way to tell which way it is growing is to go up and look at the hole. The brown-edge side of the hole will be the direction the grain is going, because when they cut the hole, they cut the roots off the grass, and the grass dies.

From Off the Green

Your putter is always an option from around the greens, given short grass and a smooth terrain. We call a putt from more than two or three feet off the edge of the green a "Texas wedge" shot. The shot was really born in Britain, on golf courses that have wide areas around greens without deep rough. I think it was widely used in Texas in years gone by, on courses that were drier than what we see today, before automatic sprinkler systems. The main adjustment you need to make is to move the ball back in your stance a couple of inches from your putting setup, which automatically sets your hands a little more forward than usual. Also, grip your putter a little more firmly. Your decision to use this shot should be based on the way the area around a green is manicured. It's a good shot to know. Use it, but don't overuse it.

The Right Speed

Speed is the most important thing you need to work on in putting. I like the idea that the ball can go in the hole from all sides of the cup. Now, that's the ideal speed! Some people are good enough that they can hit the ball at the center of the cup a bit firm and have it hit the back of the hole. But most of us aren't that good. So give yourself the best possible odds.

You need to develop a consistent feel for speed. You don't want to be hitting a putt that dies at the hole one time, then charge it eight feet by the next time.

A great practice routine is to try to get all your putts within a 24-inch diameter around the hole. That leaves a foot on either side. Whether you are putting from 10 feet, 20 feet, or 50 feet, try to leave yourself that length. The ideal is to leave the ball six inches behind the hole every time, but you can take that "never up, never in" idea to extremes, too. Remember, the putt that is rolling a gentle speed at the hole may go in from every side of the cup.

The easiest, simplest way to lower your scores is to eliminate three-puttings. There are three ways to do that: First, work on short putts: place six balls or so in a four-foot circle around a hole on a little slope. Each putt will have a slightly different break. It's good practice and will help you be a better "finisher" on the greens. Also, work on those "makable" putts from 10 to 12 feet in. And finally, don't neglect 40-footers; see how many you can roll to within that 24-inch circle. Remember, everyone can become a good putter. I think a lot of us have spent half of our lives trying to hit the ball farther. And that has kept us from working on our short games as much as we can or should. But the short game represents half your score. So it makes sense to work on it half of the time.

7

THE SHORT GAME

Chipping and Pitching

The clubhead speed and power that we all try to create in the long game isn't a factor when you get closer to the green. Distance is no longer the goal—control is. What you are looking for is the right length of stroke and tempo to the stroke. Notice I use the word stroke and not swing to ingrain that sense of tempo. A soft touch and a smooth tempo go together. Keep this in mind as we discuss pitching, chipping, and bunker play. It's a whole different ballgame.

Chipping

The best way to learn how to chip is to relate it to how you putt. Chipping is an extension of that stroke. However, you're using different clubs—clubs built to hit a full shot. I have always been most comfortable gripping down on the club to chip with. I believe it gives you more feel.

On your basic chip shot from off the green, you want to open your stance slightly to get a better view of the line and to be more comfortable swinging the club back and through to the hole. It's not a big swing, but a short, rhythmic stroke.

Set more weight on your left side at address to reduce body movement. Certainly there should be no weight movement. The shot isn't that long. This setup keeps you more or less still, but not frozen. It encourages stroking through the shot without trying to "lift" the ball in the air. Make a nice smooth stroke and let the club you choose loft the ball.

In most cases around the green—unless you are in some kind of adverse condition—you play the ball forward in your stance, meaning forward of center. Your stance narrows considerably for these shorter shots—so that your left heel is separated from the center of this stance by only a couple of inches.

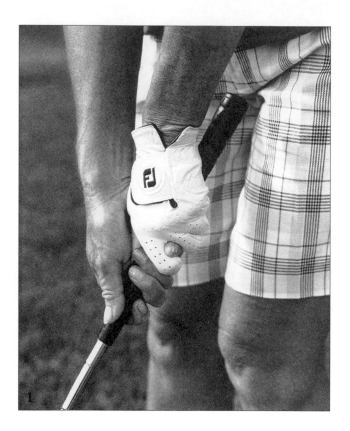

THE BASIC CHIP. *I recommend choking up on the grip somewhat for more control (1). Open your stance slightly to get a good view of the line and set your weight on your left side to discourage lower-body movement (2). It's not a big swing but a shorter, rhythmic stroke—an arm swing, with a little bit of hand action for touch (3–4). The key is to keep the club moving through impact (6–7).*

Any body motion is unnecessary—you are not trying to hit the ball for great distance. It is an arm swing from the shoulders, just like putting. But as with putting, I also recommend a little hand and wrist action to give you a sense of touch and feel. It's a "combination" stroke—of arms swinging from the shoulders and a little bit of hand action. The key to success is letting the wrists cock slightly on the backswing, and on the through-swing making sure your arms swing through with the clubhead. If your arms stop at impact and only your hands and clubhead finish, you will be very inconsistent. This is a common misconception; people think that when they are flipping their hands at the ball, the problem is with their hands. It isn't. The root cause is their arms stopping at impact; their hands react to that.

Club selection

Club selection is important in chipping and is something you should experiment with. If you have no trouble carrying the ball over and can land the

YOUR POSITION RELATIVE TO THE FLAGSTICK DETERMINES YOUR SHOT SELECTION. *You have many options in chipping and pitching the ball around the greens. What you do is largely determined by how much green you have to work with. To the shorter hole (on the left), I would take a more lofted club. To the flagstick farther away (on the right), I would take less loft and allow the ball to roll toward the hole.*

ball on the green and let it run a long way, you can chip with as little as a 6- or 7-iron.

Too often, players go wrong when they are much farther from the green—15 feet or more—and they still chip with a club with very little loft. They must land short of the green and try to run it up. That can be risky. Pros play most of their chip shots with wedges, because this makes it easier to be delicate with the shot. *When possible, make sure you land the ball on the green*—it will react more predictably. Pick a club with enough loft to allow you to land on the green. The next most important factor is "how much green do I have for the ball to roll?" More loft is needed if the hole is near. You may use less loft if it is farther away; use a club ranging from a 6-iron to a sand wedge.

Green speed is a big factor in your club choices. The faster the greens, the more you should consider extra loft.

From just off the green, you will often have the opportunity to use your putter instead of a lofted club. From the fringe, even a short distance back, the "Texas wedge," as it's called, can save you strokes. There is less chance of making a mistake—you're not going to hit the shot thin or fat with your putter. If you are more confident in your putter than any other club, use it when you can. However, don't take this to ridiculous extremes, and don't putt as a way of avoiding the chip. Learn to be an effective chipper. It's not that difficult.

Pitching

A pitch shot, by definition, has more "air time" than a chip shot. Chips have more "ground time." Because you are going to throw a pitch a little higher in the air, you normally play it with one of your wedges. It's a longer stroke than a chip, with the club coming to about waist-high. A nice smooth tempo is critical to these shots. You need to practice in order to learn to pitch the ball certain distances. A good example would be if you are 15 yards from the edge of the green. Swinging the club back waist-high, with a smooth tempo, is a good way to start to learn how big your stroke has to be for different distances.

Ball position

Play the ball forward in your stance, just inside your left heel. This sets your hands ever so slightly ahead of the ball. Setting your hands slightly forward should be exactly that. This is not a case of "if a little works, maybe more will be even better." Slightly forward creates a descending motion where the club

PITCHING THE BALL. *A pitch is a bigger stroke than a chip. Keep the ball forward in your stance at address, allowing your hands to fall slightly ahead of the ball. The club will swing back to about waist-high on the backswing, with a nice calm tempo. Swing through the shot about as far as you swung on the backswing. Your arms go as long as the stroke goes.*

strikes the back of the ball and "pinches" it. Be careful that you don't close or "hood" the clubface. A lot of people do that, taking off loft and in effect turning a pitching wedge into a 7-iron. Then they wonder why the ball comes out low and hard. It may look to your eye as if the club is slightly open. That's OK. It's preferable to hooding it and reducing the loft.

BODY MOVEMENT. *You can see from behind me how there is some lower-body movement with this shot. My hips have gone ahead and turned through the shot, and* *my body has released through impact as I throw the ball up toward the flagstick.*

If you have taken out a sand wedge or pitching wedge, and the ball comes out low and running, you are doing something wrong. Either the ball is too far back in your stance or you have hooded the clubface.

As in every aspect of the short game, it is now important that the stroke be long enough for a smooth tempo. If the stroke is too short and too quick (they go together), that can also produce a low shot. We are looking for a lofted shot that hits the ground softly and is in control.

COMMON FLAW: The most common problem in chipping and pitching is that when the club gets to the impact area, the player's arms stop and the hands try to force the clubhead through the shot. It's as if they get to the ball and their arms hit a wall—so their hands try to finish the job. You need to keep the clubhead moving through impact, and you want your arms to keep moving, too. Here's a tip I've heard all my life and still subscribe to around the greens: *Never* let the clubhead pass your hands. Your arms go as long as the stroke goes.

The lob

When you need to hit a high shot over a greenside bunker, the "lob" shot is a good one to have. It's similar to a pitch (your weight is still stabilized on your left side): Your hands are slightly ahead of the ball and the ball is placed forward in your stance. Keep the ball toward your left heel.

OPEN CLUBFACE.
This is how the wedge looks when it's open.

This wedge is square. You need to open the face to play a lob-type shot.

LOB SEQUENCE. *When you have trouble such as a bunker to carry, you should consider a lob-type shot. Open the blade and your stance, stabilizing your weight on your left side. The ball position is forward of center, toward your left heel (1 and 2).*

The key to this shot is to break your hands away from the ball sharply (3 and 4). Let your hands swing through the shot with a nice, slow swing to lob the ball up over the bunker (5, 6, and 7).

You need to open the blade, which will increase the loft of the club. Break your hands away from the ball sooner, since an early setting of the wrists will create a steeper angle—more up and down. Let your hands swing back nice and slow and full. Don't let the clubhead pass your hands. If you do that, it means your hands are overtaking your arm swing.

Remember, if you start with the blade open and make this slow, full swing—the ball will not fly very far. You're looking for height, not distance. If you hit your normal sand wedge 50 yards to begin with, you are probably looking at 35 yards. After you've mastered this, adjust the length of your stroke for different distances.

Take enough loft

If you're 10 yards off the green and your choice is to land the ball on the green, make sure you take enough loft. Too often, players use a 7- or 8-iron, carry the ball on the green, and have great difficulty stopping it soon enough. If the ball is going to land on the putting surface, it's much easier with ample loft.

I find that people are afraid of loft, especially women. They think it requires something special, or they have a general fear of hitting it fat or blading the ball. In fact, it's no harder to hit the ball solidly with a wedge than it is with a 7-iron, given a decent lie.

When people take a lofted club, they tend to move the ball back to their right foot. This takes loft off the club and turns a wedge into a 7-iron. You're close to the ball with this shot, your stance is narrow, and the ball should be positioned somewhere between your left heel and the center of your stance. This ball position allows the club to be at rest the way it was built, and will eliminate a lot of your mis-hits.

When grass gets in the way

Around the greens, you're often going to get lies where there will be grass between the clubface and the ball.

The technique for this shot is similar to blasting a ball from a bunker. It must be played with a sand wedge. Open the blade slightly and break your hands early in the stroke so it will be fairly steep. Keep the clubface slightly open through impact—don't turn it over as you would in a full shot. Go ahead and let that grass get between the clubface and the ball. The important thing is a nice tempo and a full-enough stroke. Sometimes it's a full swing, sometimes it's a half-swing, and sometimes it's a pitch-length stroke. But the mechanics remain the same. Just because you feel the grass making contact with the club, don't suddenly try to work harder with your hands to get

CURTIS STRANGE

17-time PGA Tour winner, including 1988 and 1989 U.S. Open

"A stronger grip should help women in chipping and pitching. Remember, especially if you don't play very often or you get in a tense situation: It's easier to chip the ball and get it running on the ground than trying to throw the ball up in the air."

JUDY'S NOTE: A strong left-hand grip eliminates any need for rotation in a chip or a pitch stroke. Hence, you'll make solid contact more often.

through the grass. Don't let it make you stop. Again, a key thought is to let
your left arm and hand keep moving right on through the hitting area. We're
back to that old adage: "Don't let the clubhead pass your hands."

However, don't exaggerate and get your hands *too far* ahead of the club.
When that happens, the club hits very high on the ball, and the result is a
low, screaming shot, usually to the right. The relationship you established between the club and your hands at address—with your hands a couple of
inches ahead of the ball—should be maintained through impact. If you are
comfortable playing a nice little explosion from the bunker, you should be able
to pull this off.

The bump-and-run

If the terrain allows you to land the ball short of the green and run it to the
hole, your risk of a mis-hit is greatly diminished. Play this shot with a less-
lofted club (6-, 7-, or 8-iron), with the ball in the center of your stance, and
make an elongated stroke similar to a chip-and-run from the edge of the green.
Hand action in this shot is minimal. Don't try to hit the ball very high in the
air. Your biggest risk is that you have to hope for the right bounces. It's a valu-
able shot to have in the wind.

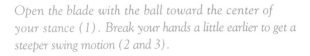

Open the blade with the ball toward the center of your stance (1). Break your hands a little earlier to get a steeper swing motion (2 and 3).

Through impact, keep the angle of the clubface open—don't turn it over as in a normal shot (4). Go ahead and let the grass get between the club and the ball. But keep the club moving through the grass—don't stop!

The lie of the ball

Your options and the choices you make chipping and pitching are largely dependent on your lie. When you get a more bare lie, it's more difficult to use lofted clubs; 6-, 7-, and 8-irons are easier to play with. Never use your sand wedge from very firm, hard-packed turf. The flange and the bounce on the bottom of the sand wedge dictate that you need a little cushion of grass under the ball. The flip side is, when you're in long grass, regardless of the lie, a less lofted club won't work.

A final thought on saving strokes around the greens: Don't put too much pressure on yourself or think you need to knock every shot close to the hole. You can learn to chip it up close so that you only have a short putt left, or you can hole a nice putt from 10 to 15 feet. Either way, you've gotten "up and down" with your short game.

8

BUNKER PLAY

You Don't Need Dynamite
to Escape the Sand

Bunkers scare most golfers, and the higher your handicap, the more you fear them. This is understandable, in part because it's a different kind of a shot from any other you face. It's often described as an "explosion" shot where the force of the sand being "blasted" propels the ball out of the sand. But I think that's a misnomer. These words imply you need dynamite to get out of the sand! But if you ask good bunker players, they will tell you it is not a violent act at all. There is a lot of rhythm and tempo to it and, in most cases, the longer, more fluid stroke produces a softer, better shot than a hard stroke. The only time there's any real force involved is when the ball is buried.

It is actually easy to get the ball out of the bunker, because all you need to do is slide the club under the ball, letting the sand throw the ball into the air. There's a slight margin for error in bunker play, because the club does not contact the ball directly. It's not always easy to get the ball close to the hole, but I can guarantee a way out of the bunker if you're willing to practice it.

One early fear that must be overcome is opening the clubface. This increases the effective loft, but most of all it makes the club function better in the sand. It's somewhat frightening to do, but it's one of the principles of bunker play. You have to have the courage to open the blade to play these shots correctly.

Equipment matters. You are going to need a sand wedge with a little bounce on it. The flange or sole of a sand wedge is exaggerated, and as that sole becomes more curved at the bottom, the "bounce" of a particular club is increased. Aside from loft, the sole of your sand wedge is what sets it apart from other irons in your bag. (There are photos illustrating the degrees of bounce in sand wedges in Chapter 11.) Sand wedges with the

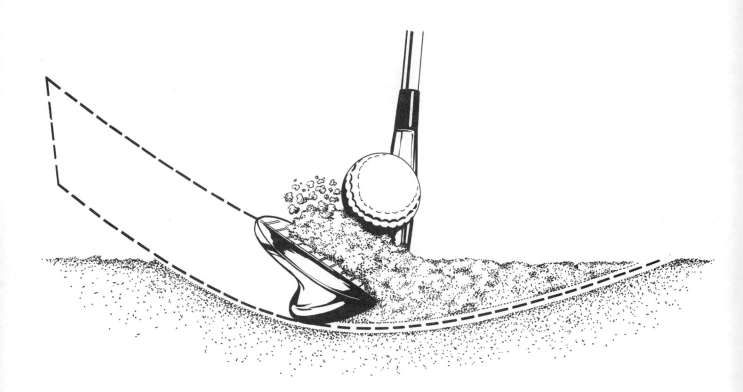

FROM THE SAND, THERE'S NO CLUB-BALL CONTACT. *The bunker shot is the one time in golf that the club does not contact the ball directly—it slides underneath the ball if you execute the shot properly.*

most rounded bottoms make bunker play the easiest but are not as useful from the grass.

The basic design of a sand wedge, though, helps the club to slide through the sand under the ball and not dig into the sand. Digging is deadly in a bunker, and encourages the sort of violent stroke that we would like to avoid.

Setup

You want your weight braced on the left side of your lower body with your stance open and the ball forward of center, almost to your left heel. You must work your feet into the sand for good, firm footing. (Sometimes this will also give you a sense of the texture and weight of the sand in the process.) Your upper body has to feel as though it's set up behind the ball. Grip down on the club slightly and hold the leading edge of the clubface about halfway up the golf ball. You cannot ground your club. The resulting position would have your left thigh and your left hip braced ahead of the golf ball, and your

THE BASIC BUNKER SHOT SETUP. *Brace your weight against your left side and open the sand wedge at address.*

shoulders and your head slightly behind the ball. This is what enables you to avoid digging into the sand—and is the key to allowing the club to slide under the ball and to throw the ball high into the air. Remember, your lower body is braced to the left, and your upper body is set behind the ball.

Greg Norman once talked about bunker play as requiring a sort of "splash shot." I like that choice of words. Another good analogy is that you are just trying to feel as though you are going to throw some sand out of the bunker with the clubhead. Some of the better bunker players really don't take that much sand. Again, we're getting away from the idea of an explosion shot. Good bunker players take a consistent amount of sand, somewhere between an inch to two inches, behind the ball. But they have an instinctive feel for how long their swing must be for different distances. The less sand you take, the more control you have over what you do with

Break your wrists as early as you can on the backswing to create a steeper angle for the return to the ball.

HOLLIS STACY

18-time LPGA Tour winner, including three U.S. Women's Opens

"Opening your stance promotes the steeper angle you're looking for in bunker play. As shots get longer, I square up a little more to get the swing more U-shaped.

"I always aim at the same point behind the ball, regardless of the length of the shot. When practicing, I try to create square, smooth divots in the sand. This tells me my sand wedge is doing its job."

JUDY'S NOTE: As bunker shots get longer, the steepness of a stroke becomes less important, and squaring your stance will help you to carry the ball farther. As we recommended earlier, Hollis adjusts the length of her shot with the length and speed of her swing—not by taking more or less sand.

THROUGH IMPACT.
See how the blade does not turn over until well past impact.

DISPLACEMENT OF SAND "SPLASHES" THE BALL OUT. *The club never actually makes contact with the ball—it's the displacement of sand that "splashes" the ball out of the bunker and onto the green.*

the ball. Examples of this type of player on the tours are Curtis Strange, JoAnne Carner, and Sandra Palmer. And it's the way I play bunker shots. It takes a lot of practice to learn the right combination of swing length and speed and how much sand you should take—but it's time well spent.

A lot of people teach that the club has to go outside on the backstroke and across the target line to the left coming through a bunker shot. You want to keep the blade open through the shot, not turning over the clubface as you would with a normal full shot. The outside-in swing does help people to keep the blade from turning over. However, with a very strong grip, as I have, taking the club outside away from the ball is difficult.

I achieve the same thing by breaking my wrists up as early as I can. This creates a steeper angle for the return to the ball, and the club can slide under the ball without my hands turning the clubface over. At impact and just past, the clubface is in the same position it was at address. If your left hand and arm continue through the stroke past impact, the blade will not turn over. If your clubface turns over, you'll dig into the sand and you'll have trouble getting out of most bunkers.

FACE ANGLE STAYS OPEN. *Through and past impact, the angle of the clubface remains the same.*

Much later in the through-swing, the hands and arms have begun to allow the face to turn over.

TRY THE "SPOT" BUNKER DRILL. *You can learn how to hit good bunker shots. Draw a line a few inches behind the ball. This is the point where the club should enter the sand. Try this as a practice drill.*

Watch the pros. A soft touch and a smooth tempo go together. There is never any effort to suddenly pick up speed. They take a fuller, rhythmic swing. You really can't swing too full in a bunker. You can swing too hard or too fast or too short, but you won't make too big a swing as long as your tempo fits the length of your swing. Hollis Stacy has been one of the game's great bunker players—and tempo is her biggest asset.

The spot technique

I learned my bunker play as a child with the "spot" method. You look at a spot behind the ball and hit to it—or through it. You might want to start with this simple method, or return to it if you're having trouble with bunker play. All you do is draw a line in the sand, a couple of inches behind the ball. You want the club to enter the sand at that point and have it slide under the ball. The ball will then be splashed out. Try it in a practice bunker with and without a ball, just working with the line in the sand. Remember, there won't be any practice stroke on the golf course. It's against the rules to ground your club in a bunker—it's a hazard.

Slopes and Angles

If you find yourself with an uphill lie or a downhill lie or even a sidehill lie in a bunker, your normal method will work well only if you can set your body with the slope. For instance, in the front of a bunker, you'll often find yourself on a severe uphill slope. At address, your left leg becomes much shorter than your right leg. Allow your hips and your shoulders to accommodate the hill in the same way. This encourages the club to swing along the slope.

In a reverse situation with a severe downhill lie, not only will you accommodate the hill with the angles of your feet, hips, and shoulders, but you'll want to break your wrists and arms up even more sharply to be able to swing along the slope.

When the ball's above you, hold your sand wedge very "short," depending on the severity. Otherwise you risk taking way too much sand.

In the case of a ball way below your feet in a bunker, it's most important to maintain, throughout the stroke, the flex in your knees that you've established at address.

Buried Bunker Lies

If you don't have to carry the ball very far and there is room for the ball to run to the hole, put the ball well back in your stance and close the clubface—you want to "hood" it shut, decreasing the loft. As you swing, cock your wrists, breaking your hands up very sharply (that's the thing I emphasize most about bunker play—break your wrists early). This, combined with your arms swing, gets you ready to hit *down* behind the ball and go through it as hard as you can. Don't be afraid to hit down behind the ball with a fair amount of force. The worse the lie, the more aggressive you must be. When you do this, the ball will come out hot and running, but you will be out of the bunker and putting.

I repeat: You can only play this kind of shot when you *don't* have a great expanse of sand to carry and you have room to let the ball run.

Here's a shot if the ball is buried near the edge of a bunker, with the hole close to you. It was taught to me many years ago by Larry Mowry, a former LPGA Tour rules official and mini-tours player who scored a great triumph in the 1989 PGA Seniors Championship. Keep the ball forward in your stance as you would in a normal bunker shot and the blade slightly open. Break your wrists up sharply on the backswing, and when you hit down behind the ball, *leave the club in the sand*. The action of the club not following through makes the ball "pop" out a little higher than normal, and makes it land softly and "dead." The ball won't run far—it doesn't have overspin—but you have a chance to get it relatively close to the hole.

If you cannot play one of those two shots, you have to consider playing out in a different direction, sometimes away from the hole. A lot of today's

FROM A BURIED LIE WITH ROOM TO RUN THE BALL OUT. *Put the ball back in your stance, right of center, and close the clubface in this situation (1). Break the hands very sharply going back (2 and 3), and then hit down behind the ball and go through it hard (4, 5, and 6). The ball will not carry a long way and will come out running hot. So this shot works only when you don't have a great expense of sand to carry and have room for the ball to run when it lands on the green.*

FOR A BURIED LIE WITHOUT ROOM TO SPARE, LEAVE THE CLUB IN THE SAND.

When the ball is buried near the front edge of the bunker and the hole is close to you, you should keep the ball forward in your stance and keep the blade of the sand wedge open (1).

Make your normal bunker stroke with the hands breaking early (2).

newer courses have bunkers so large and/or deep that if you should get a miserable lie, it can't be played forward. That's when you have to make a good decision and look to save the most strokes. You might have to play the ball out sideways and hope you can hit a good pitch and get up and down.

The "Chipping" Alternative

One thing that you may need to do when you have a long distance to the hole, no lip to deal with, room to let the ball run, and a good lie, is to "chip" the ball out of the bunker. This makes sense, particularly since so many courses have huge greens. Take an 8- or 9-iron and grip down on the club—making it a little shorter. (This is a little insurance for picking the ball clean.) Put the ball just back of center in your stance and your weight to your left side,

But when you hit down behind the ball with some force, leave the club in the sand—don't follow through (3 and 4). This action will make the ball "pop" out and land dead

without much spin. So it won't run nearly as much as the closed-clubface shot would. From this second angle you can see how forceful this shot is (5 and 6).

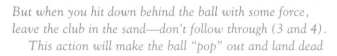

CHIPPING IT OUT.

When you have a very long distance to the hole and can run the ball toward your target, you might want to "chip" the ball out of a bunker. Take less loft—maybe an 8- or 9-iron—and grip down on the club. The ball position is back in your stance—right of center. The key to this shot is eliminating body movement. It requires a little arm swing and hand stroke to make clean, crisp contact with the ball. There is no displacement or splashing of sand involved here.

eliminating body movement. It's a little arm swing and hand stroke. If your lower body moves, you won't contact the ball solidly. If you keep your body quiet, you can get out safely by "picking" the ball clean from the sand.

Fairway Bunkers

Restricting lower-body movement is the key here, too. It has got to be more of an arm and upper-body swing. The biggest cause of problems is excessive lower-body movement, which will almost always cause your feet to move in the sand. You ensure a mis-hit when that happens.

First, take one more club than you normally would from this same distance. Grip down on the club an inch or so as you settle your feet firmly into the sand. Ball position doesn't vary from what you would normally do with your chosen club. Remember, you want to hit the ball cleanly.

The swing itself is a shoulder turn and an arm swing, with your legs and feet more still than usual. You're not going to contact the ball as well as you would from the fairway, but you might save a stroke if you can hit the ball flush from the sand.

Stronger golfers can play a "ball first and through the sand" method from fairway bunkers, much as you would from nice turf. But, I have rarely seen that work well for women.

For most people, this shot should be played with either a 6-, 7-, or 8-iron or a lofted wood, depending on the distance and the severity of the bunker's lip. Forget long irons.

Someone once said, "A bunker is not a place of pleasure." Remember, it is a hazard. So my best advice is to try to stay out of them, and take the fewest risks when you are in one.

FROM FAIRWAY BUNKERS, CHOOSE THE RIGHT CLUB AND REDUCE LOWER-BODY MOVEMENT. *For women especially, don't try this shot with anything less than a 5-iron. You need a utility wood (left) or a lofted iron (see the photo sequence beginning on page 124).*

If you use an iron (page 124), take one more club than you normally would and grip down on it for a little insurance (1). Ground your feet into the sand to help stabilize your lower body (2). Although my lower body appears to move (4, 5, and 6), it is really quite restricted compared with my normal swing. When your feet start moving too much on this shot, you're in trouble.

The shot itself is more of a shoulder turn and arm swing, and you want to "pick" the ball clean from the sand.

1

Choke up on your club.

2

Dig your feet in.

5

6

Pick it clean from the sand.

Restrict lower-body movement.

You're out!

9
SPECIALIZED SHOTS—
TROUBLE AND
OTHERWISE

Living with the Wind

Adjusting to conditions and recovering from trouble are essential to keeping your scores down. That can be particularly difficult when the wind kicks up. It's not always a lot of fun. A golfer friend of mine coined what could be the title of a golf book by Erma Bombeck: "When the wind isn't blowing, it's very tough to iron." In other words, when you get a beautiful calm day, you don't want to spend it indoors doing chores! But spending the last 28 years or so in west Texas, I have learned to live with the wind. Shorter people and flatter swingers like me have an advantage, too. The taller you are, the more upright your swing becomes naturally—and the more the wind will wreak havoc with it.

Whether the wind is "with" or "against" you there are problems that you need to minimize. Many people look forward to having the wind at their backs, presuming it's going to be fun and easy. You've turned the corner on your golf course and suddenly you're going to be hitting less club and it's going to be a breeze. Here you are hitting a 7-iron 130, 20 yards farther than usual. However, it doesn't always turn out that way. Being downwind tends to quicken your tempo and push you toward the target, because it becomes more difficult to complete your backswing.

Everyone has a position at the top of his or her swing that is a "set" position—a spot that tells us we can change directions in a smooth manner. If you start to change directions too soon, before you are set, your upper body gets ahead of the ball, moving laterally toward the target. This is something some golfers fight anyway—thinned or topped shots result.

Concentrating on completing your backswing can solve these problems. Make sure you get it to the top and don't cut it short. In addition to getting you set at the top, this helps get your upper body behind the ball, producing more solid contact.

You might be surprised to know that the wind at your back can often beat the ball down and not lift it and make it carry farther. Solid contact will help you to hit the ball higher downwind and, as a result, have more control of it.

The other thing is to trust your club selection. Often you don't trust the wind to change the length of the shot. You try to hit the ball harder, and you hit a shot that lands hotter than a tamale and runs out of control. So don't try to swing harder—just focus on contact. The best wind players are successful because they are able to make their normal swings and hit the ball very flush.

Into the Wind

Deciding which club to hit is even trickier when hitting into a strong wind. Most people assume they'll get 10-yard increments between their clubs: They hit the 5-iron 130 yards, the 6-iron 120, and so forth. But if you are a woman player who drives the ball under 175 yards, you will probably get smaller increments—7 to 8 yards—between clubs.

When you're playing into a wind of 15 to 20 miles per hour or more, your normal distance guidelines go out the window. The gap narrows to about half of your normal readings, to four or five yards between clubs, maybe as few as two or three if you're a weaker player. You need to be aware of this. Too many people take just one more club than normal and then try to kill it. Listen to the pros sometime when they're playing in a British Open or on a day when an ill wind blows. A severe wind is the one thing that can really inflate scores. You'll hear the pros say things like, "I hit a 3-iron there where I'd normally hit a 6." And I'm talking about big strong guys. If they have to make those kinds of adjustments, so will you. Always err on the side of taking more club than you think you need into the wind. I was an excellent wind player, and taking plenty of club into the wind was a factor.

Adjustments

After you've made a good club choice, move the ball a couple of inches farther back in your stance than you would with a normal address position. To hit a ball that has some character into the wind, you want to feel a little bit

LOW BALL INTO THE WIND. *Ball back in stance.*

Takeaway.

A three-quarters backswing.

Returning to the ball.

Staying low through impact.

Hands turning over through the shot.

Head releasing, eyes following the ball.

Abbreviated finish.

tighter in your wrists, so that the end result is a three-quarter-length back-swing and a three-quarter wrist cock. This method will help you avoid the most common error into the wind. Golfers often think that hitting down on the ball harder and more steeply will help keep it low and out of the wind. It doesn't. Striking down on the ball harder from a steeper angle actually makes the ball balloon up in the air. And the ball rarely reaches its target when it balloons upward.

What you need to do is apply the same technique that comes naturally to a flatter swinger like myself. The angle is less steep coming back to the ball and the club travels parallel to the ground longer past impact. In other words, the club goes from impact to along and through the turf, not down and into the turf. You don't want to dig; as with bunkers, digging is death. So think parallel to the ground and through the turf, not down into it. Paul Azinger is a player who excels at this. He has a long, flat area through and past the ball. That's one reason he hits the right kind of "boring" shot into the wind.

The Rough Stuff

When you get in the rough, it is a good idea to move the ball back in your stance a bit and grip down on the club. As the club gets shorter, it becomes easier to swing it a little steeper—which is what it takes to successfully escape from the rough stuff.

You want to hit the ball with more of a de-scending blow. So break your wrists earlier in the swing to help create that steeper angle. You also need to firm up your grip, because the grass is going to wrap around the hosel, and as the club slows, it will turn the face over. You'll hit a blue-darting hook of some sort when that happens or never get the ball airborne.

JoAnne Carner is one of the most successful LPGA players in history, and she had a real advantage in the rough because her strength, and a naturally steeper swing, allowed her to recover better than many women players. Jack Nicklaus is the same. His more upright golf swing made

FAIRWAY WOOD FROM THE ROUGH.
For most women, lofted woods work much better from thick rough and poor lies. You don't want to try to get out of this stuff with a long iron. Break your hands up sharply, as I have here, to create a steeper angle of approach, and be sure to swing through the shot.

him able to recover from deep grass. It's no coincidence that both of these players compiled stellar records in U.S. Opens, where rough is taken to an art form.

Because you'll be creating more of a descending blow, it will probably produce more of a left-to-right shot, so you need to allow for that.

My experience—and just about everybody's I know in women's golf—is that from very poor lies in thick rough, we've been more successful with lofted woods than we have been with long irons. That's why I advocate carrying a utility wood in your bag. This is a highly lofted club with a heavy sole designed to cut through deep grass or help you escape other bad lies—divots and so on.

When it's really thick, impossible rough, you've got to pay the price. Simply take a lofted iron—maybe even a wedge or 9-iron—and hack your way back into the fairway. Don't get too greedy, because even a mid-iron does not have enough loft to always get the job done. The pros have to swallow their medicine when this happens—and so, painful as it is, do all of us.

Bad Lies

When you get a poor lie near the green—the ball is nestled down in deep grass instead of sitting up—you have to make adjustments. Put the ball slightly back in your stance. Break your wrists a little quicker—you are trying to get steeper in your swing. You need to eliminate as much grass between your clubface and the ball as possible.

It is important that you don't take your hands and try to shovel the ball out of the bad lie. You should let your arms swing through, leading your hands and letting the clubhead do the work for you.

Be logical in these cases. If you have a lie that you can't pop the ball out of, then hit a shot that is going to allow the ball to run. As you gain more experience, you'll know which lies are playable and which aren't. The best thing you can do if you have a poor lie around the green is to hit a shot that is going to stay on the ground. If you can possibly run the ball from a very poor lie, there is much less risk.

As your skill level improves, you'll have more confidence and need to bump and run the ball from some lies much less often. But until then, stick with the safest possible shot—and run the ball when it's necessary.

Unusual Lies

Golf courses aren't entirely flat, and you often encounter some rather unusual lies, with the ball either above or below your feet. Logic dictates that regardless of the type of hill you are on, you need to adapt your setup to that slope. Your goal is twofold: to make your club swing more easily along the slope, and to keep your balance.

Punching Out of Trees

A big part of being a player good at getting out of trouble is making the right decisions. You have to know when you can go and when you need to minimize your losses and play back to the fairway. Once you've made the decision to go for it, avoid flinching in mid-swing. The smallest little move can make the clubface vary just enough to make you hit the tree that you would have otherwise missed by three or four feet.

It's paramount that once you've made the decision, you put your mind on the business at hand, which is to execute the shot. Quit worrying about the trouble and the trees. In fact, if you watch the pros on television, you will notice their heightened powers of concentration and how they are often able to pull off some of the most amazing shots in these situations.

Low shot

The technique for a low punch is very similar to the kind of shot you would hit into the wind, although more abbreviated. In most cases, if I have to hit the ball from under a tree, I'm going to take a club without a lot of loft. I'm going to take a 3-, 4-, or 5-iron, regardless of the distance. I always grip down on the club, because I need to put the ball back in my stance to start it out low and to keep it low. I am much more comfortable doing that—the swing works a lot better. I grip down on the club a half an inch to an inch when I move the ball very far back in my stance. This is one of a few specialized shots where the ball moves back slightly right of center.

With the ball back in your stance and your hands low on the club, you'll find that your hands naturally fall quite a bit ahead of the ball, and that your weight is slightly braced to your left side. The loft of the clubface is reduced. Check to make sure your clubface is square instead of, as is often the case, opened when your hands are set far ahead. This common flaw is why many players lose the ball to the right of their intended target. If you're

Uphill lie: The ball should be more forward in your stance. Brace slightly against your left side. Allow for a draw or pull.

Downhill lie: The ball should be back in your stance. Break your wrists earlier on takeaway. Allow for a cut or push.

Ball below feet: Get much closer to the ball. Flex your knees more and bend at your hips as necessary. Stay down through the shot and allow for a fade.

Ball above feet: Get slightly farther from the ball. Grip down on the club to make your swing adapt to the hill. Allow for a hook.

THE LOW PUNCH
THROUGH TREES.

This shot is similar to the into-the-wind situation. Grip down on the club and put the ball back in your stance. The clubface must be square at address. It's a three-quarters swing, very controlled. And you want to keep the club low through impact and beyond, with a low finish. Concentrating on exactly what you need to do to execute the shot—and not focusing on the trouble or the trees—is something that better players excel at when faced with these predicaments. Your chances of escaping from trouble will be much improved if you can narrow your focus as the pros do.

trying to weave the ball between trees, not having the clubface square at address is fatal.

This address position encourages the kind of swing you want to make—a shorter, three-quarter backswing. Your wrist cock is firmer and about three-quarters as well. As the club comes back through the ball, your swing and your address position will encourage the club to stay low and parallel to the ground longer than in a normal shot. You are trying to keep the club low through impact and beyond. Your hands won't feel nearly as active through impact, and your finish will be shorter and lower than with a normal swing.

If you become proficient at this, you'll find that hitting a low shot that turns from right to left is relatively easy. Turning the ball left to right is more difficult. It requires a very strong left side and a left hand and left arm that really keeps moving through impact and doesn't allow the club to turn over. The very things that encourage the cut also encourage height. It's a difficult shot to play even for very good players. They will tell you that the low cut is one of the more difficult shots in golf.

High shot

When you need to hit the ball high, you make different adjustments. Move the ball more forward in your stance because you're trying to catch the ball ever so slightly on the upswing. At address, you might want to tilt your weight slightly to your right—but don't overdo it, because that will make it difficult to hit the ball solid. Just move the ball forward, keep your head down, and be sure to swing through the shot. The tendency here is to try and lift the ball, and that results in a thin shot that doesn't go very high at all. Stay down through impact. It's a full swing and a high finish, not an abbreviated one like the low shot described above.

Hooks and Slices

You won't always be in trouble when you find a need to work the ball one way or another. I never change my grip to play either of these curving shots. I believe you're able to work the ball in either direction mainly with adjustments in your setup. The appropriate changes alter your swing path through impact and allow you to hit the ball right to left or left to right.

The hook (right to left)

The most basic adjustment in your setup is at your feet. Aim slightly to the right of your target and then draw your right foot back, closing your stance. Allow your body alignment to follow—your knees, hips, and shoulders. This encourages your swing path back to the ball to be more from the inside, swinging through impact slightly right of your target. If you don't interfere, this path encourages your hands, arms, and the clubhead to turn over and create right-to-left spin on the ball. Don't confuse this intentional, controlled hook with a shot that starts to the left and then hooks—a pull hook. That is the result of an over-the-top move—a bad golf swing. To effectively draw the ball, you must have the courage to start the ball to the right of your target.

SET UP FOR A HIGH SHOT. *When you want to elevate the ball, move it forward in your stance and tilt your weight slightly to your right side. From there, it's a nice full swing and high finish.*

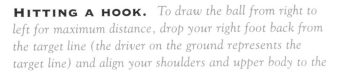

HITTING A HOOK. *To draw the ball from right to left for maximum distance, drop your right foot back from the target line (the driver on the ground represents the target line) and align your shoulders and upper body to the* *right of the target line (1). Swing back to the inside of the target line on the backswing (2). Be sure to allow your hands to turn the club over past impact, which will make the ball hook toward the target (3 and 4).*

The slice (left to right)

Your setup should be the reverse of that for the hook. Aim slightly left of your target and draw your left foot back, opening your stance. Allow your body to fall in line—your knees, hips, and shoulders. This setup promotes a little straighter takeaway or even just to the outside, and a swing path that returns to the ball more on the line to the target and swings through to the left. This swing path discourages a releasing motion and keeps the clubface slightly open through impact, creating left-to-right spin.

A shot that starts to the right and then slices is commonly known among good players and teachers as a "block." It results when the club swings down the target line and tension in your left hand and arm doesn't allow you to ever release the club. Remember, the slice that you can control and that is effective will start to the left of your target.

If you need to exaggerate either one of these shots, adjust the clubface at address. For the hook, close the clubface by turning the toe of the club slightly in; for the slice, open the face, setting the heel slightly forward.

THE CUT SHOT.
Although most people are trying to get rid of their slice, there are times when you need to curve a shot from left to right. The basic setup is with an open stance and open hips.

Swing the club across the target line with the hands turning over much later after impact. Think "delayed release."

10

EXERCISE

Warming Up and Stretching Out

At my peak I was one of the best female players in the game. I weighed 107 pounds. But I was not weak. The best way to gain strength for golf is by hitting balls. I know this sounds obvious, but I used to find that I'd lose hand strength during the off-season, simply because I wasn't practicing as much. You can power-lift and exercise all you want, but there is something about buckets of balls that strengthens your specific golf muscles. There is no substitute, and it's a lot of fun—or can be.

However, I must also strike a cautionary note: You don't want to whip out the driver first thing. You need to warm up and loosen up, and should start with the shortest, heaviest club in the bag—a wedge or sand wedge—and hit some little half-shots. Then hit some full wedges, move on to a mid-iron, and gradually work your way up to the driver. You need to get your muscles stretched up and loose, kind of like a major-league pitcher who starts out throwing at slow speeds and gradually starts popping full fastballs.

Warming up for a round of golf is really a matter of getting your muscles stretched out and getting your hands to feel nice and comfortable on the club. This is not the time to get bogged down in mechanical thoughts and different little moves you are going to make—although if you are working on something, you can continue to work on it then.

Stretching

Not all the warming up comes on the practice range. It's good to stretch before you begin hitting balls. I'm talking about some simple stretching exercises. I could get very complicated here and give you dozens of things that would make you a good mate for the Incredible Hulk, but I know you are not going to do those things more than twice. So I'll stick to things that I think golfers can and will actually do. It's counterproductive not to do any warm-

SHOULDER STRETCH.

Hold a single golf club at both ends and lift it above your head. Then put it over your shoulders and behind you.

up. Some people think it means arriving at the club an hour earlier, and use the excuse that they don't have the time to warm up properly. But it can be done in 15 to 20 minutes, and every little bit helps.

One of the most common stretching routines is to take a wood or long iron in your hands, holding it at each end—by the head and up by the grip. Now take the club from the front of you, up to the top of you and then all the way over the back. It's a good shoulder and arm stretch to get you going. I don't think there's anything magical about it, and even though it looks pretty difficult to get the club behind you, I've never seen anyone who couldn't do it. Or take two clubs and swing them back and forth slowly. They sell weighted clubs for this purpose. That extra weight stretches you out a little bit.

Health clubs have long wooden poles, maybe five or six feet long and quite light in weight. I put that pole over my shoulders and turn back and forth. Due to the length of the pole, I can coil twice as big with my upper body as I can without it. It exaggerates my ability to turn with ease. I don't think it hurts any of us, particularly women, to increase the amount we're

WARM UP BY SWINGING A COUPLE OF CLUBS. *Swinging two clubs at a time is a good way to loosen up your golf muscles on the first tee. Even if you* *don't have time to do much else, do this before you hit your first tee shot.*

TURN, TURN, TURN. *With a club behind your back, turn back and forth. Because so much of the golf swing throws your weight in one direction, from left to* *right, stretching out in all different directions keeps your body in balance—and helps to prevent injuries.*

STRETCH YOUR HAMSTRINGS BEFORE YOU TEE OFF. *You can stretch out against a wall or the side of a golf cart. Just hold on to the sides and lean forward, one leg and then the other. Keep your heels down!*

able to coil from the waist up. Like everybody else, I'm getting older, and I find that with age and after back surgery, I don't turn as fully or as easily as I once did. Doing this kind of stretching and coiling, with a pole or with a golf club, really helps.

Hamstring stretches are a very good idea before any physical activity, including golf. Your hamstring muscles are connected all the way from your ankles to your neck. They have a lot to do with a healthy, flexible back. With golf, we are constantly throwing our body, in the midsection of our spine, in one direction—from right to left. So keeping everything stretched out becomes even more important. You need to take particular care of your back. And the best way to do that is to keep your muscles stretched.

If you have particularly tight muscles or a little backache, you might want to do your stretching in the ladies' locker room as close to the time you're going to start swinging a club as possible. You don't want to do it an hour and a half beforehand. Sometimes I just lean against a wall, a bench, or a golf cart, put my arms against it, and stretch back and forth with each leg, as shown in the photos above. It's a runner's stretch.

BEND DOWN AND AROUND. *From a basic golf posture—with knees slightly bent and feet spread apart— bend over from the waist and let the weight of your upper body stretch out your leg and back muscles. I do this and then turn and do the same thing side-to-side against each leg. Don't do this with your knees straight, especially if you're a bad-back sufferer.*

THE FINGERTIP
PUSH-OUT. *If you can do*
real fingertip push-ups, great!
If not, stand a couple of feet or
so back from a wall with your
fingertips bracing you against
it. Now lean up against the
wall, keeping your heels down
as you go forward and
backward. Not only are you
stretching out your hamstring
muscles—but you are making
your upper body, hands, and
arms a little stronger as well.
It's a two-fer.

All the things that make your muscles a little longer are going to make you swing the club more easily.

Doctors and physical therapists will tell you not to bend your back with your legs straight. And being a longtime back pain sufferer, I'm pretty careful about things like that. A warm-up stretching exercise I like to do is this: With my legs apart and a little knee flex like I would have in a golf swing, I bend over and just let my hands and arms hang down freely. And then I stay that way for 10 seconds or so. Let the weight of your upper body hang free so it stretches out your lower-body muscles.

When I feel that those muscles are kind of loose and have stretched out, I'll then turn to the outside of each leg. This seems to get all the area around my hips, thighs, and back a little bit looser before I hit golf balls.

Remember, don't try this with your feet together—you could hurt yourself. And don't push your muscles to the point of pain.

As a young person, I learned to do regular push-ups from my fingertips, which helped build up my fingers, hands, and arm muscles. I don't do that anymore, but I do a kind of fingertip push-up against the wall. Get far enough from the wall so your body weight makes a difference, at least two feet. Keep your heels down, and when you go forward, not only are you stretching your hamstrings, but you are making your upper body and your hands and arms a little stronger, too. Try it.

All the top players do a lot of stretching. Greg Norman is unbelievably flexible because of the stretching work that he does. Stretching makes you stronger and more supple, and it helps you to avoid injury.

You see a lot of tour players in the fitness trailer working on the Stairmaster and trying to strengthen their lower bodies. The addition of the fitness trailer on the LPGA Tour has played a big part in so many women professionals gaining strength seemingly overnight. Distance averages range from around 260 yards for the longest hitters to around 235 for average-length players.

Long-distance walking is a very good way to build your lower-body muscles, too. I'm talking four or five miles a few times a week. And it's not

"GET A GRIP"—GET A GRIPPER! *One of the major differences between men and women golfers is in the area of hand and wrist strength. You can develop that by getting a ball to squeeze or an individual finger-exerciser like the one I'm using here. Work with your gripper in your spare time, like when you're stopped in traffic or at a traffic light. Hand and wrist strength comes naturally to some men as a result of their athletic backgrounds. Women who have not been particularly athletic are at a real disadvantage here when it comes to golf, so you have to work at it—constantly.*

stressful on your whole body, like running. I highly advise walking when you play golf, too. It not only gives you an element of exercise, but I believe it helps you play better than cart-golf does.

Hand Strength

One area that is probably a weak spot for most women is hand strength. Men develop it as second nature; women don't always. It is developed by a lot of little things, including hitting golf balls. A practical tool is a little hand-gripper. They're like balls that you squeeze; they even have one now where you can work each finger individually, like playing a trumpet. Get one and keep it in your car. When you come to a red light, do your exercise for a minute or two. It'll strengthen your hands and help pass the time more quickly.

I don't recommend sit-ups for golf, but things that make your stomach muscles stronger help protect your back, and that's wise for golfers.

You can go to a workout room a hundred days in a row, but if you never hit a golf ball, I am not sure you are developing strength that will translate to your golf game. It really takes a combination of both. For a person hell-bent on getting stronger, hitting balls four or five days a week is about as good a way as any.

But you need to make a distinction between a practice or training session and warming up. You don't need a whole bucket of balls to warm up; you can do a lot with 20 to 25. And don't skip the practice putting green. Roll a few putts, at least one a 30-footer, to get accustomed to the greens that day. Having rolled a few putts is certainly going to keep you from wasting strokes on the first couple of holes.

All of the warm-up advice and strengthening suggestions here take a minimum of time. And it is time well invested.

11
EQUIPMENT

It Can Help, If You Get the Proper Fit

Some women think that because they don't play particularly well, equipment isn't very important to them. They couldn't be more wrong. Equipment is especially important for the poorer and physically weaker player, because getting the right clubs and balls can help this player more than anything. Tour players—both men and women—are highly refined athletes whose touch is more developed, and they can tell the difference in equipment more easily than can weekend players. But basically, they can play reasonably well with anything; that's not necessarily the case for the average golfer. The more you know about equipment and the better you know your game, the better chance of getting a set of clubs that fits you.

Many women simply are uninformed about what clubs they have, what's available, and what their alternatives are. Some just take whatever their husbands give them, accepting hand-me-downs or whatever they can get their hands on. That's OK to an extent. You can take your husband's metal driver and try to cut it down for yourself, or even for a teenage child; that might work, because it probably won't be way too heavy. But you cannot do that with a set of irons, because you'll come out with a very short, stiff, heavy set of clubs that will never allow you to improve very much. So at some point, you need to get clubs that are right for *you*!

Experimentation has been the key for me in my career. I started playing men's-length golf clubs when I was about 12 years old, and I was a fairly little girl growing up. I weighed 80 pounds at age 14. I wanted longer clubs to get more distance. Bob Green, the pro at our course, always helped my father to get clubs that fit me, and that makes a big difference in how you develop. You can get into a lot of bad habits playing with your father's driver that somebody cut seven inches off of. It's one way to start, but a bad habit to get into.

When you go to buy clubs, you should rely on people who are in the business and know equipment. That usually means your local pro or an expert at a golf shop, or even an off-course store specializing in golf. If you go into a general sporting-goods store and buy golf clubs, you might be taking more of a chance. You are at their mercy and you have to hope that the person selling the golf clubs has some expertise. He or she may not. In that case, if you have a friend who plays well or who knows anything about the game, take him or her with you. The safest thing to do is go to a good pro shop and tell them this is a once-in-several-years investment and that you're interested in both the best clubs on the market and also something that fits you and would give you the best chance to progress.

Set Composition

Set composition is a critical area for women, and one everyone must grapple with. It's nettlesome because our greatest needs generally fall on the two extremes of the spectrum—the longest clubs (drivers and woods) and the shortest clubs (pitching and sand wedges). So how many woods should you carry and how many wedges? You can carry only 14 clubs. Because they are the hardest clubs to hit, you should eliminate the long irons—the 1-, 2-, and probably even the 3-iron. Wedges are used a lot by women, because we tend to be short of so many greens! There are two basic types of wedges—the pitching wedge and the sand wedge, used mainly but not exclusively for bunker play.

You need a pitching wedge that is just part of your set that goes 8 to 10 yards shorter than your 9-iron. And the basic sand wedge for getting out of bunkers is essential. From there you need to determine how many "spaces" are left in your bag and how many extra sand wedges you could use. One of the keys to wedge play is learning exactly how far you can hit a full sand wedge. I know I personally have a gap of 30 yards between my sand wedge and pitching wedge, and I would like to close that gap.

Grip Size

Grip size is very important, and sometimes overlooked. You need a grip that fits you—after all, this is the only contact you actually have with the club, so it must be right. If a grip is too small, you may find that you can't hang on to the club. The same is true if the grip is too big. If you have average-size hands, this might not be much of an issue with women's clubs. Manufacturers are getting better at catering to the women's market, but sometimes you get grips that feel as if they're for children. They mistakenly think all women need little grips, and that's just not true.

Too small a grip tends also to make your hands overly active. Too large a grip inhibits hand action. Large grips are helpful for arthritic hands, however.

If the grips don't fit properly, they're fairly easy and inexpensive to change in a pro shop or repair shop. If they don't feel right, check with your pro. You can get every grip in your bag changed for less than $40 (it's about $3 a club).

Don't wait until your grips get hard and slick with age. That creates a lot of extra tension in your grip so that you're fighting to hang on. You need grips that let you hold the club with a nice comfortable grip tension, not constantly feeling like you're going to "lose" it. You should replace your grips every couple of years at a minimum, depending on how often you play.

Shafts: Stiffness and Kick Points

Graphite shafts were a huge boon to women, and you see a lot of them on the Tour. Now they're making steel shafts that are similar in weight. But before graphite, everything was heavy. The lighter overall weight allows the less physically endowed player to swing the club faster, and it has allowed manufacturers to enlarge the clubheads. I definitely feel women golfers should play with lightweight shafts. The flex also needs to be considered; nothing in the stiff range makes sense for anyone but the strongest, male players. The more flexible L or R shafts are where you should be looking to start.

The biggest part of fitting is getting a shaft that is right for you. It's not just how much a shaft flexes, but where that "kick point" might be. The kick point is the area in the shaft—either lower, center, or higher—where the shaft actually does most of its flexing. In recent years, shaft manufacturers have developed more shafts with higher kick points. As the kick point gets farther away from the weight of the clubhead and nearer to your hands, the shaft will feel stiffer and react like a stiffer shaft. Almost all women seem to do better with shafts with lower flex points. I know I can swing a fairly stiff shaft with a low flex point. If the flex point comes up higher, I can't handle it at all. Ask your pro.

Take advantage of all the test clubs offered at golf shops and consider trying a friend's clubs. As your level of ability improves, experimentation with shafts is even more desirable and productive. If you are a beginner and/or

JAN STEPHENSON

16-time LPGA Tour winner, including the 1983 U.S. Open

"I think all women should have graphite shafts in their clubs. Any woman today that doesn't have graphite is giving up too much yardage. Because graphite shafts are lighter, you can generate more clubhead speed."

shorter hitter, someone with some club knowledge can usually fit you with a playable set of clubs.

Weight and Speed

Companies are finally coming out with good women's golf clubs. The dead-weight or overall weight of the club is far lighter than it used to be. At the same time, the standard length is longer than in the past; they are making women's drivers with a standard length of 43 inches. A few years ago, that was *the* standard length for a men's driver.

Remember, distance is a product of mass and speed. So what we are really talking about is the weight of the clubhead coupled with the speed you can swing it. I can take a clubhead that weighs next to nothing and swing it very fast, but because there is no mass, I don't produce much distance. Or I can take a very heavy golf club—you might think this big thick mass might propel the ball a long way—but I swing it so slowly that there's no benefit. So what you want is the heaviest mass that you can swing and control at the fastest speed. In my early 30s the fastest I swung a driver on a machine that tested impact was 96 mph. I could consistently measure 93 mph.

The best driver I ever had was 44 inches long and weighed 11.6 ounces, which in terms of drivers is a very light club. I was able to create a lot of clubhead speed, and I'm sure the same would be true for you. Be careful, though, not to get a club that's *too* light. You have to be able to feel the club-head and have a sense of where it is.

Swingweight is a measurement that relates the weight of the shaft and the grip to the weight of the clubhead. Its most important function is to ensure consistency throughout a set of clubs. I can say pretty confidently that the low end of the swingweight spectrum for women should be about C-4 and the high end D-0. Once you play golf at all, you will develop a feel for what the clubhead is doing. If a club is too light, you will also have trouble playing with it in the wind. To me, the ideal club for everyone is at the lighter end of the spectrum but with enough weight to provide clubhead feel.

Drivers

The driver is the club we tend to focus on the most, and it is very important. The new, big, oversize drivers do make driving much easier. I don't know that they necessarily help you to hit it longer, although for everyone there

BOB ROSBURG

ABC on-course commentator and 1959 PGA champion

"Women more than men need a driver with a lot of loft—12 to 13 degrees is what I recommend. And there are even some cases where a 3-wood from the tee goes farther, because it's easier to get in the air and you can carry the ball farther.

"Women tend to play a lot of their golf early in the mornings when the fairways are wet and there's a lot of dew on the course. Under those conditions, you're not going to get a lot out of the ball on the ground—so you need to drive it in the air."

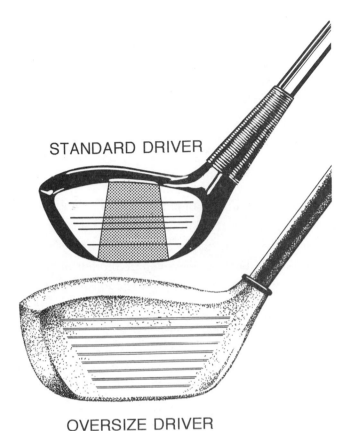

STANDARD DRIVER

OVERSIZE DRIVER

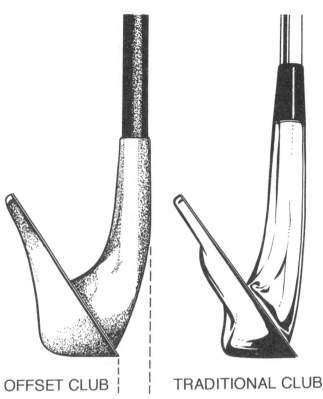

OFFSET CLUB | TRADITIONAL CLUB

OVERSIZE VS. STANDARD DRIVERS.
Drivers are getting bigger and longer in terms of their clubface hitting area and the length of shaft. Lightweight materials such as graphite have really helped this happen without adding to the overall weight of the club.

The oversize or big-headed metal drivers (bottom) seem to help players make solid contact and get the ball airborne. The wood-wood (top) traditional drivers that I grew up with seem to be passing from the scene, but they're still solid, reliable golf clubs. You should experiment with different lengths of drivers, shafts, and designs to find the combination that clicks for you and allows you to generate maximum distance.

OFFSET VS. TRADITIONAL IRONS. *Golf clubs that are "offset," with the shaft or hosel of the club not running in a straight line into the clubface, are designed to help the average golfer get the ball airborne. They've become predominant in the market and are recommended for beginners.*

seems to be a combination of a big metal head and shaft that suddenly makes them hit the ball a bit farther. The larger clubhead simply makes it easier to make solid contact and to get the ball airborne, because of the way the weight is distributed. If you have trouble with your tee shots, you should definitely look into them. And make sure you've got enough loft on your driver;

few women should play with a driver that has less than 10 degrees of loft. If you are a pretty consistent ball-striker, a good experiment is to try a driver with a shaft that is one-half to one inch longer than your present club. Extra driver length helped me to hit the ball farther, whereas less loft or more weight never did.

Irons

As for oversize irons, in all honesty I don't see much benefit. They obviously have a larger hitting surface, much like the larger tennis racquet. For the lowest skill level, it should make the game easier. Irons became larger a few years ago and that made a difference, but the new oversize models may have gone over the edge. Clubs have to suit your eye. I grew up with more traditional clubs, and my eye still likes to see the nice straight line of the shaft running onto the leading edge of a clubface. Today it's hard to find a club with that look, because most clubs are offset to help players get the ball in the air (see illustration). When you look down the shaft, you are going to see the leading edge of the blade fall behind the shaft. Most players are used to it by now, I guess, but for me it still looks a bit odd simply because I grew up with traditional, forged blades.

The perimeter-weighted, offset clubs undoubtedly benefit a lot of people and are widely used on the LPGA Tour, the Senior PGA Tour, and, to some degree, the PGA Tour. They certainly help most golfers in minimizing off-center hits. The also help in elevating the ball. You will still get more feedback from a traditional, forged iron. But that's not the way the market is going. I will probably never play a forged iron again.

Lies: upright vs. flat

A big issue for women is the way irons sit at address. Women of average height often get clubs that are too upright. It's not such an issue with the woods, but if an iron doesn't sole reasonably well so that neither the toe is up in the air nor the heel is off the ground, you are going to have a hard time hitting good, solid shots. A good test is to address the clubs on cement, and you can more easily see if the bottom of the club soles right for you. You have to stand on your tippy-toes to properly sole a club that is too upright. You can take clubs into a repair shop and get them bent so that they sole properly. But it's better, of course, to get them right from the start. Get an expert to help you fit the lie of your irons. It's very important, and it dramatically affects your ability to hit the ball flush and straight.

LIE MUST BE RIGHT. *It's critical that the lie of your irons—the way they sit when soled on the ground—fits you. The angle of the graphite-shafted club (in my right hand) is more upright (for a taller player); the angle of the steel-shafted club would suit a player shorter in stature.*

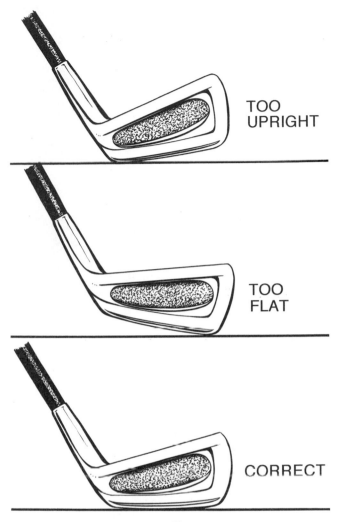

TOO UPRIGHT

TOO FLAT

CORRECT

CHECK YOUR LIES. *If you set your irons against concrete, you can check to make sure the lie is right—not too upright (top, with toe in the air) or too flat (heel of club in the air). A professional can help you to get equipment that fits you properly.*

Sand Wedges

Many women could use two sand wedges, one with more "bounce" (a larger, rounded sole) for getting out of bunkers and one for playing from the turf. But we may not be able to afford that luxury, because we need the lofted fairway woods in our bag.

Again, you need to do some experimenting to see if you have a "gap" from, say, 50 yards in, that you need to close—or if you really need more help

THE SAND WEDGE.
This club is built differently from the others in your bag, with a sharper angle of the clubface between the leading edge and trailing edge. The curve between those two edges is known as the "flange," or bounce, of the club.

SAND WEDGES AND FLANGE. *Sand wedges come with various amounts of "flange" on the bottom. On the left is my sand wedge, with a minimum of flange and bounce. The middle sand wedge has somewhat more, and the one on the right has a big flange and bounce. The average woman will need one with plenty of flange and bounce for sand play, but this kind of club has its limitations from turf.*

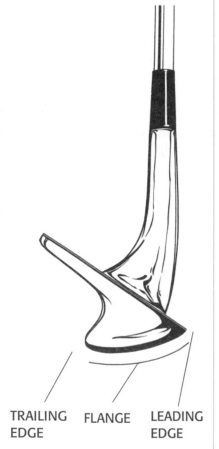

TRAILING   FLANGE   LEADING
EDGE   EDGE

from right around the greens, maybe with one of the higher-lofted "L" type wedges with as much as 60 degrees of loft. One of the secrets to successful wedge play is knowing exactly how far you can hit, say, a full pitching wedge or sand wedge. Very few club players I know are good at taking that club and hitting it full at the flagstick and getting it close. Not so with professionals. They know within two to three yards where that ball is going to land. Very often when they lay up on a par-5 hole, they calculate precisely how far they want to leave themselves for a full wedge shot. You'll hear it on TV all the time. I hit my sand wedge probably somewhere between 70 and 75 yards, and 72 is probably about right on the money. How far do you hit yours? Find out—it'll help in pinpointing your equipment needs.

Utility Woods

If you find you don't need a third wedge, there are all sorts of specialty clubs to consider—especially utility woods. Aside from the driver, a 3-wood, 4-wood, or 5-wood, almost everyone can benefit from one of the higher-lofted "utility" clubs. These can replace a 2-, 3-, or 4-iron and save you a little stress. I am now looking at a 7-wood myself. Some of these clubs come with a sole with rails that really help to advance the ball out of the rough, something many women need help with. These clubs can do so much—you can hit it out of deep grass, out of divots, off bare lies, from the fairway, and from fairway bunkers. To be honest, I don't see how many women or average golfers can play without one. I'd suggest the ideal set composition for a woman would be a combination of four to five woods, definitely including a utility wood, eight to nine irons, and a putter. There's a lot of room for variation and experimentation within those parameters. The greater your skill level, the more options you'll have.

RAILED SOLE HELPS FROM THE ROUGH. *A good utility club is a must for a woman. With railed soles, the club is especially helpful in getting the ball out of the rough and fairway bunkers.*

Putters

Putters are much more a matter of personal preference and style. They sell more than anything, as single items, because people love to try out new ones (especially after a bad putting round), and there's no shortage of magic wands to choose from. Clubs have to look good to your eye, especially putters. What you want, finally, is a putter that you're most comfortable with and gives you the most confidence, especially with alignment.

There are many different styles: straight blades, mallet-head putters, off-set-hosel putters such as "Ping," heel-shafted putters, center-shafted putters—you name it. It seems to me, after many years of experience and observing putters, that a center-shafted putter works for more people. The best putters, people who are innately gifted, putt well with heel-shafted putters. That's why you might see a lot of them on the tour, but that doesn't always mean they're right for you.

A center-shafted putter doesn't mean the shaft falls in the center of the putter blade. But basically, it is not heel-shafted. Experimentation, again, is the key. Putters are fun to try out, and once you get one you like and can get some confidence in, voilà!

The ideal length of the putter is somewhat dependent on your height and the length of your arms, as well as how you stand to the ball. Do you prefer and feel more comfortable with an upright putting stance, or farther away from the ball? There's more on this in the putting chapter, but these factors affect the length of putter you'll want. Probably most women are going to find that a 34-inch putter is about the right length for them; 35 is a little long, and 33 a little short. But those are just general guidelines.

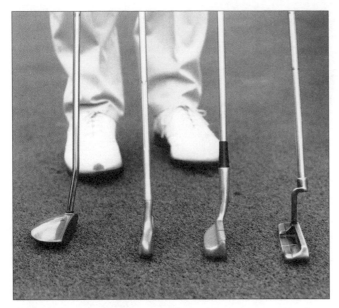

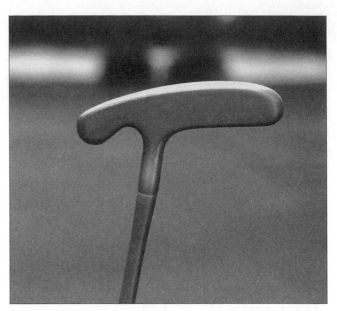

FOUR BASIC STYLES OF PUTTERS. *Finding a putter you're comfortable with and that suits your stroke is largely a matter of taste. These are four of the most basic models: (from left) mallet head; traditional Bull's Eye; heel-shafted, flanged-blade, Armour-style putter; offset hosel, "Ping"-style putter.*

CENTER SHAFTED IS NOT DEAD IN THE MIDDLE. *"Center shafted" doesn't mean the shaft runs straight into the center of the putter. This putter is also considered center shafted, even though it's more toward the heel of the blade than the toe. The bottom shows what we usually consider a rocker sole; this accommodates different heights and posture.*

SHAFT ANGLE FOR UPRIGHT OR FLATTER STYLE. *The angle of the putter shaft should be more upright for someone who prefers to stand erect and close to the ball (outside putter with graphite shaft and ball against blade). For someone who stands farther from the ball, the shaft should be more angled and the blade somewhat tilted. This angle will produce more of a circular stroke.*

Alignment aids are on many putters, such as Zebras, etc. The best putter is one that you can most confidently align well. I can't tell you what type that is going to be. But if you believe that you are setting the clubhead down where you are looking, then you are going to be a better putter. Alignment aids sometimes help in this regard. If the line on the putter isn't helping you to aim right where you want the ball to start, it is not worth anything. If it helps, or if you think it helps, by all means, use a putter with an alignment aid.

Golf Balls

There are two basic types of golf balls among the many you'll find on the market: wound balls and those made of two-piece construction. The wound ball has rubber windings around the core and comes in different compressions. Most often, they have a softer balata-type cover, and the feel is softer. These are targeted toward the better players, many of whom believe these balls perform most consistently, and they can spin them more. But things are getting confusing these days, because two-piece balls with harder covers are being made to spin and perform more like the old wound balls. Two-piece balls are the balls of the future, particularly now that manufacturers are making two-piece balls that are easier to stop. In general, average golfers are better off with the two-piece ball to begin with, and the reasons are economic. These balls are more durable, because their covers do not cut or scuff easily. And two-piece balls certainly perform, distance-wise. If you are just beginning, obviously the two-piece ball makes sense for you. And you don't need to buy the most expensive balls on the market by any means.

However, there are trade-offs you should be aware of. That little bit of distance you may gain with a harder, two-piece ball off the tee may cost you strokes around the greens. The two-piece balls that get the maximum distance are harder to spin, and they can be difficult to control around the greens. If you play on a particularly hard, fast golf course and shots around the green are difficult for you to control, you may have to consider using a softer, wound balata-covered golf ball. There are now two-piece balls with softer covers offering more spin, so they're worth trying, too. The more accomplished a player you become, the more the ball will make a difference to you. We've seen some examples—Payne Stewart being a notable one—of a player who changed balls because of an endorsement contract and had difficulty adjusting. Nanci Bowen won the 1995 Nabisco Dinah Shore, though,

ROBERT GAMEZ

1990 PGA Tour Rookie of the Year

"The easiest way to gain distance is to simply change equipment. That's all I did; I went to a big-headed driver and the two-piece Precept ball and picked up yardage off the tee. You've got to experiment a little to get the right club and ball, and make sure you've also got the right shaft in your clubs."

with a harder two-piece ball on very firm, fast greens, so these balls can perform in extreme conditions.

Some golfers become infatuated with the idea of spinning their approach shots, trying to make the ball "suck back" on the greens as you sometimes see the pros do. Sure, it's neat to see a golf ball dance in a way, but backspin isn't realistic for the average golfer, particularly the woman who is trying to advance the ball all she can. You want overspin and forward roll, not backspin. Softer landings on greens will serve you better. As my friend Bob Rosburg likes to joke, most people can't get it there, so why do they want it to stop?

Compression—a measure of the ball's hardness—can be confusing, too. There's a macho-image thing about it for some who want to play a 100-compression ball like the male tour players. Well, that's a little silly. Some of the strongest players in the world on the men's tour are playing a 90-compression ball. So again, it becomes a matter of how it feels to you. There is even some argument that compression is a fantasy of sorts, merely a marketing device. But for the average woman player, even the better woman player, the 100-compression ball is not an issue. Forget it. I don't think the 80-compression ball makes much sense, either. The 90-compression ball works for most people most of the time.

Golf Gloves

You have the choice here. You certainly don't have to play with a glove. But for most people, it tends to give a little bit better grip and more security. Many right-handed people who play golf right-handed find that a glove on their left hand makes it feel more stable. I'm so dominantly right-handed that when I put a glove on my left hand, it gives my left hand more importance and makes it feel more solid. But I have played with a glove almost all my life, so in my case it has become habit. It will for you, too. If you don't want to make the investment in golf gloves, don't ever start wearing one, because you will get used to it and you will need it.

12

THE LPGA TOUR

Competition and Opportunity

I've been around the LPGA Tour since the early 1960s. I came straight out at age 17, without stopover for college, and competed for 22 years. You live a little bit of a yo-yo life as a touring professional. Your score is in the paper every day for all the world to see. There is that daily elation or humiliation level about golf, and you tend to define yourself in terms of what you shot or how you're playing. You win and lose a little bit every day. If you're winning more than you're losing, you're having a pretty good time. But not many people do that. Still, it beats just about everything else I know of as a way to make a living. But that's not to say it's easy.

The vast majority of players coming out onto the tour these days come from college programs. Title IX, mandating equal funding for women's programs in colleges, has given women's sports and golf a big boost, along with the overall boom in the sport in the last 10 to 15 years. Today's players come out with a good deal of maturity and experience that helps them tremendously. I remember when I first got on tour, I was very intimidated playing alongside the Mickey Wrights and Kathy Whitworths, and it took me a while to feel I belonged. There's still a period of adjustment—Brandie Burton told me she felt the same awe for a while. It's tough for polite young people to be respectful, enjoy their youth, and know they still have things to learn, and yet be confident and assured about their talent and ability. The arriving LPGA'ers are now much more seasoned in competition. And they need to be, because unlike for the men, there aren't that many attractive alternatives if you can't qualify for the LPGA Tour. Other tours exist around the world—Europe's is the strongest—but they still have a short season and not a lot of money. The LPGA Tour draws and features the very best women golfers, from America and around the world.

If you want an idea of how good these players are, just go out to your local club or course and watch golfers come and go. At almost every course you go to, you will see a few men players that appear good enough that you think, "Maybe he could have played the tour." But you have to go to five or six courses to find a single woman player that you would think the same thing about. This tells you how very special those who make it to the tour truly are.

Scholarships and Support

College programs are giving women the opportunities that men have had for a long time. Think about it. If you have a young child who has a slight interest in golf and can do well in high-school competition, there's a very good chance she might be able to get a college scholarship, at least a partial one. Because there are a lot more scholarships available and fewer girls in the pool going for them, it is a tremendous opportunity, and being active and athletic is becoming more and more acceptable all the time among women. This won't necessarily lead to a career on the LPGA Tour. But it will help subsidize a college education, and that's something worth pursuing given the staggering cost of higher learning these days.

However, I must make one point here. There's something I see in golf, and I would bet it has some basis in all of women's sports: There are many women I know who think we should have equal opportunity with men, but a lot of those women don't, in fact, physically or financially support women's sports. For our daughters and granddaughters and all the young people coming along to realize equal opportunity, we have to become equal supporters of women's sports. It can't be just lip service.

Unfair Comparisons

In many ways it is unfortunate that the LPGA Tour has so often been compared with the PGA Tour and now the Senior PGA Tour. Because the men's tours have been what we could rightfully call phenomenal successes, nothing can compare to the growth they've experienced. If you look at the growth of the LPGA Tour in the last 20 years, compared with anything else—like a major corporation—it would appear to be just what it is: a very viable, successful organization. In 1995, the LPGA Tour played 38 events for more than $24 million in prize money. When I came out in 1962, we played 32 events for a total of under $400,000 in prize money.

The LPGA likes to call itself the most successful women's sports organization in the world, and I believe it is. A handful of tennis players are mak-

HELEN ALFREDSSON

Winner of 1993 Nabisco Dinah Shore championship

"I think we need to get the message out to women that it's OK to be an athlete. You can do other things, too. But it's a tough balancing act out here. It's hard trying to be pretty, trying to be feminine, trying to be skinny, trying to have your hair done nice, having long nails—and then hitting the ball 300 frigging yards. I mean, put that equation together. It does *not* work."

ing millions, but golf supports far more people. And there's a crucial difference: Women's tennis is able to piggyback its major championships by playing them concurrently with the men's events, at the same sites. Women's golf has really survived on its own, and today it is undeniably thriving at the professional level as never before.

Not so many years ago, it was not that hard to be a consistent money winner on the LPGA Tour. You could probably name the people who were consistent tournament winners. As the talent pool has increased, the depth on tour has also become much greater, so that today there are many more people vying for those big checks. There's always the addition of one or two great players every generation, but now there are just so many more *good* players out there. And they seem to be physically stronger and, in fact, much taller than the players of my era were.

Evolution

We are getting to the point where the average height on the LPGA Tour is in the 5'8" to 5'9" range. That is a pretty tall average. I see that as an evolutionary change. We are not going to see players like Patty Berg, Louise Suggs, Marlene Hagge, and Sandra Palmer (all successful at 5'2" in earlier eras) continue to be successful at the pro level in the future. That doesn't mean you can't be a very nice player, play the game well, and enjoy it. There is an exception to every rule, but if you're 5'2" and going against players who are 5'10" or 5'11", your margin for error is going to be so much less that the odds are stacked against you. If you are taller and stronger, you should be able to use that to an advantage. But if you are not, it doesn't mean that you can't play. Patty Sheehan is 5'3". The excellence of her play, consistency, and course management have put her in the record books, with the 1992 and 1994 U.S. Women's Opens among her accomplishments.

The LPGA Tour also teaches us that good players come in all shapes and sizes. We're not all tall, muscular, big women. Nobody could have been much more average in size than I was at the peak of my career. I was 5'4" and 107 pounds.

The average golfer can learn a lot by watching the LPGA Tour pros. Our margin for error is small. A mistake might cost me the ability to get to the green in regulation. A mistake (like missing a fairway) will mean less to a male pro; all he has to do is hit a different club from the rough. So I'm not allowed as many errors as John Daly, based simply on the strength factor. Thus, you see a lot of swings on the LPGA Tour that are technically very sound, where people are swinging the clubhead very nicely and letting the club do a lot of the work for them. Brute force isn't going to do it for us.

Don't get me wrong. I would never turn down physical strength if it were magically offered to me. I believe it makes the game easier—provided you have good mechanics—and more fun. But not being strong did not keep me from being a top player and hitting longer than average during my playing career.

There is, unfortunately, another hurdle for women: A young woman can be extremely talented, very competitive, and all those things that you want an athlete to be, and that you need to compete; but some of those things that make you a great athlete and competitor we will never accept as the way a nice young woman should act socially. And it's tough. It's tough because certain things are necessary to being a good competitor and laying it on the line every day. This is a lifelong endeavor for these women, and it means everything to them. You need to be tough at times, to be a fierce, stone-faced competitor, to get the job done.

Having It All

Just as there are some women in the business world who have it all, combining family and children with their career, so too do an increasing number of golfers on the LPGA Tour. It wasn't always that way. When I had my son, Tuey, at age 22, there were only a couple of other women players with kids out there. It wasn't easy. With the advent of the day-care center and other amenities, today's LPGA Tour is allowing women the opportunity to "have it all"—to be successful athletes and raise a family at the same time. The great thing is, we now have choices!

As the tour has gotten bigger and more financially rewarding, it's become a little more of a serious business, too. That's life. In every endeavor, as the money gets bigger and bigger, the makeup of a group and how they relate to each other inevitably changes. There's not quite the closeness there was in my day, although the LPGA is still a pretty small—and happy—family. It's been my good fortune to be a part of it for more than 30 years now.

Nine Who Taught Us All a Little Something

I am reluctant to rank players. I never saw Babe Zaharias, who is widely considered one of the all-time greatest woman golfers, hit a golf ball. But here's a list of nine who stood out in my time and taught us something about how to play the game.

Mickey Wright

Mickey Wright was the greatest ball-striker I've ever seen. She had a beautiful, rhythmic swing that was timed to perfection. She was a wonderful long-iron player. She did not excel at all parts of the game, however. She was only an adequate putter and was not a great wedge player nor especially good in the wind. But that's because she didn't have to be, and she didn't work much at those things. She was the female version of Ben Hogan, always working on perfecting her golf swing. She was such a perfectionist that mentally it may have taken a toll that kept her from winning even more often. Gene Littler once said Mickey had the best swing he had ever seen, man or woman. She set the standard for how well a woman could strike a golf ball.

Kathy Whitworth

Kathy Whitworth, on the other hand, I would not deem a great ball-striker. She was a great *player* who could do a little bit of everything. Most of all, she knew how to get the ball in the hole. She had an instinctive sense for the game, the sort of thing you can't really teach someone, and a great touch around the greens—even though you rarely saw her practicing those shots. She just knew how to get the job done, and she became the LPGA's all-time tournament winner. She even surpassed Sam Snead's record for professional victories, winning 88 tournaments.

Nancy Lopez

Nancy Lopez was the best female putter who ever played the game. She was a good all-around player, but I wouldn't call her a great driver, a great iron player, or a great fairway wood player. But she knew how to play the game and she was a magnificent putter. She was quite a long hitter and may have been the first very good player who knew how to take advantage of it—and had the courage to take chances. She was already confident as a teenager. Time has taken a small toll, as has having three daughters, but she is still very competitive at age 38.

When Nancy arrived on the LPGA Tour in the late '70s, she gave the tour a huge publicity boost by winning five tournaments in a row. She had that indefinable star quality that draws people toward her. That's something you can't teach and can't quite explain, either; some people just have it. Nancy did. She still does.

JoAnne Carner

JoAnne Carner had one of the all-time great golf swings as a young amateur when she was known as The Great Gundy (her maiden name was Gunderson). The beauty of her golf swing lessened in her professional years, but not her ability. JoAnne drove the ball a long way, and her strength was an asset in helping her from rough situations. But she never tried to hit her irons a long way. If anything, she would back off her irons a bit and not try to hit them "full value." That's a lesson for a lot of people. I think it helped her get the ball close to the hole and make a lot of birdies. And she always had so much fun playing golf that she attracted a following as well. JoAnne had and has the wonderful trait of being able to laugh at herself. We won the National Team Championship in 1977. Playing with her was a treat!

Laura Davies

Laura Davies is the longest hitter I've seen in women's golf. She is what you would call a natural. She has not had any formal lessons. Her golf swing has what appears to be a certain amount of wild abandon to it. But she does a lot of things right in her golf swing, including having what I consider just about the ideal backswing length. Because of her strength, she sometimes can't help trying to go for things that are within her reach, and that makes her fun to watch. But sometimes, a little more caution would help her down the stretch. She's lost a few tournaments by miscalculating, but who hasn't who's ever contended? She plays and wins all over the world. I think she's still maturing and learning, and she will be a force on the tour for as long as she wants to play.

Beth Daniel

I've been taken with Beth Daniel since she was a teenager when I first met and played with her. She has this great build for golf, tall and willowy, and has always had a classic tall-person's, good-looking golf swing. She can hit the ball high and far. She also has a fiery temperament that gets her up and down and even angry now and then. It might have kept her from doing even more, but she's done a lot in golf, and she is still going strong. Beth was in the forefront of the modern-day players, whose combination of sound mechanics and great talent brought more strength and length into the women's game.

Pat Bradley

Pat Bradley has an enduring golf game and has won tournaments in three decades. She went through as bad a slump as I've seen a top athlete go through in the mid-1980s, intertwined with a serious health problem. But she came back from it to excel again, and that says a lot for what's inside her. Pat manages her game very well and plays within herself, which is why she's lasted a long time. She is not outstanding in any one area of the game, but she's very capable in all areas, kind of like a Tom Kite. Her strength is that she has no weaknesses.

Patty Sheehan

Patty Sheehan has this kind of picture-book swing that is easy to admire. She is a shorter player in stature, at 5' 3", and that has hampered her ability to hit long irons as high as some players. This should give hope to all of you—here's one of the best woman golfers in the world. She is an accurate driver, an excellent short and mid-iron player, and a solid putter.

Aside from her fine swing, I admire how Patty has handled her emotions. Just two years after completely collapsing, physically and emotionally, in a U.S. Open, she came back to win the Open in a playoff over Juli Inkster at Oakmont in one of the gutsiest displays I've ever seen.

That performance gave new meaning to what women are capable of. I'm not talking just about the caliber of golf—for two players to shoot 280 (four under par) at Oakmont, one of the toughest courses in the country, was quite a milestone in my mind. And it was the U.S. Open, arguably the toughest tournament to win and the one that Patty desperately wanted. I've always been a great believer in the observation that women are more emotional than men, yet I don't believe that necessarily has to hold you back. It's just one more thing that you have to overcome in order to perform well and excel. And Patty did that.

Betsy King

Betsy King is an interesting case study because she played the tour for a long time without winning. She looked as though she was going to be just a middle-of-the-road type of player who would earn a decent living. I give her tremendous credit for the hard work she put in to get over the hump and become a consistent winner.

Betsy's golf swing was a little bit different. She approached the ball with a posture more like that which we see in men—more over the ball with her arms hanging perpendicularly to the ground. That gave her a steeper swing, and she struck down on the ball more than most women do and was capable of hitting higher shots into the greens and spinning the ball more than most. She never had too many qualms about what people thought of how she did it. For example, she gets down behind the ball with her putter to line up putts, as many beginners might do. Many golfers might have been so self-conscious that, even if this worked for them, they wouldn't have done it. Not Betsy—if it works for her, she does it.

There are many other players I could cite for their accomplishments. But let's just say there are about 10 others I would call standouts—players who had something a little special. Most of their records speak for them.

Some of the youngest, brightest stars on the scene today—Dottie Mochrie, Helen Alfredsson, Michelle McGann, Kelly Robbins, and a handful of others—I'm sure will be documented in someone else's book a few years down the road.

13

TELEVISION

What I've Learned, and What You Can Learn from It

I've been working for ABC since the 1984 U.S. Women's Open at Salem (Massachusetts) Country Club, and I've been covering men's golf since the 1985 U.S. Open at Oakland Hills in Birmingham, Michigan. Most of my work has been on the ground, as an "on-course commentator," but I've also been up in the booth on occasion, at our LPGA events. They're completely different roles. On the course, my job is to appraise what the player is facing, give the basic facts of distance and club selection, and offer quick observations of conditions and how the golfer is doing that day. Up in the booth, you're called on to analyze and put things more in perspective. You're reacting to, as much as reporting, what is happening. It was an adjustment for me at first, because I broke in as a rover and was a little reluctant to give my opinions, but I enjoy the opportunity to do both. Believe me, it is not always as easy as the network professionals make it look!

But I've learned a lot by doing television, and you can learn by watching the pros in action and seeing how they handle different situations.

Criticism and Feedback

The power of television can be a bit scary. It's a balancing act when you are dealing with people in your profession, people who were your friends before you went into the booth and—you hope—will still be your friends afterward. As a commentator, you have an obligation to be candid and honest—to call a bad shot a bad shot. It's a fine line to walk. I would never intentionally try to hurt another athlete, and I don't think any announcers would. But it can be especially sensitive when a player is struggling and blows a tournament, as can happen. I've been there for some monumental collapses in the U.S.

Women's Open, by Patty Sheehan in 1989 and by Helen Alfredsson in both 1993 and 1994. It was painful to watch, and difficult to describe. I've also seen some spectacular stuff. I was there when Raymond Floyd, someone I had known and played some golf with, broke through to win the Open at Shinnecock in 1986. I was with Greg Norman in the 1989 British Open at Royal Troon, where he birdied the first six holes and shot 63 the last day. He just played unbelievable golf, and still did not win the championship. It was hard to fathom that someone could play that well and *not* win, but he made a couple of costly errors in the playoff and Mark Calcavecchia carried the day.

Most of my relations with players are cordial and friendly. They understand I have a job to do. But sometimes you can ruffle feathers. I recall working an LPGA Skins Game one year in which I described Jan Stephenson as the shortest hitter among the four players competing. That was on the Saturday telecast. Well, Jan heard about it (she must have watched a tape of the telecast), and before the Sunday show, she confronted me about it and was angry about what I had said. I explained that, in comparison with the other three, she was the shortest. I did not say she was short. It was simply a statement of fact. She accepted my reasoning after a while. Vicki Goetze, who joined the LPGA after a phenomenal amateur career, is also getting a little weary of people talking constantly about what a short hitter she is (*Golf Digest* even did a cover story with experts telling her how to gain more yards). At some point, you start to think, I wish someone would focus on something besides the fact that I don't hit it as far as everybody else. I would give Vicki and everybody their due in that regard.

The one thing that no one can get angry with you about, best friend or not, is if you are simply being honest and stating fact. Fortunately, most pro golfers will say, "Have you ever seen a worse shot than I hit there today?" They're pretty honest with themselves. So usually it works out fine. As in most cases in life, honesty is the best policy, and if you have the facts to back you up, somebody can't be mad at you for too long.

Risk Taking

A crucial difference I've observed between the men and women on tour is that men are more risk takers, and more creative in their approach to trying shots. Women, from my experience, want more of a sure thing. If we have not practiced and perfected a shot, we think, "I better not try this." Men have more of a daredevil attitude.

I got an excellent tip from Brent Musburger when I started working with him in the ABC booth. He was talking about my hesitancy to say something. We were riding back to our hotel after a telecast, and I shared with him some of the best things I knew. He'd ask why I didn't use that on the air and I'd answer, "Because I wasn't exactly sure," or I'd say, "Well, it's just my opinion." He urged me to say what came to mind. In his words: "Go ahead and throw out what you know. Once in a while, you'll be wrong, but not very often."

He was right, and I think that applies to golf, too. To get better at the game and to have fun playing it, once in a while you have to take a little chance; and with success you will find that pretty soon it isn't a chance anymore.

You can't spend your whole life playing safe, and part of the fun of golf is trying to pull off the impossible. But you need to be prudent when the odds are stacked mightily against you, too. You can see how players size up a situation in deciding whether to "go for it" or not. I don't think much commentary is called for in these situations; the microphones that pick up the conversation between a player and his or her caddie often provide the best audio.

Learn by Watching

As a viewer, you're seeing the players on or near the top of the leaderboard, so most of them are playing well, obviously. Mechanically, you can simply watch players and imitate. It helps to pick players who have a build somewhat your size, and they come in all shapes and sizes on the LPGA Tour. Notice the rhythm with which players swing the club, how easy they make it look. They repeatedly demonstrate the truth of what Bob Toski used to say: "It's a game of effortless power, not powerless effort."

In the short-game area, it should be clear how touch and feel come into play. Certainly it doesn't take a guru for somebody who plays golf a little bit to watch some of the good things that they do. One thing that you will notice is that every good putter I can think of, other than Nancy Lopez, has very quiet hands. And by quiet hands, what I really mean is quiet wrists. That is very evident when you watch pros on the putting green, especially when the camera zooms in on the grip for one of those terrific close-ups. Watch Patty Sheehan's quiet hands, for example, and her smooth-as-glass stroke. This is the kind of thing you can take from a telecast and go right out to the golf course and try.

What you get mechanically is one thing, but what you absolutely should take advantage of seeing is how the pros approach certain predicaments, because they face some of the same problems that you face at home playing on Tuesday or Wednesday, only to a greater degree. They can do more things with the ball than you will be able to do. LPGA players can't do all of what Jack Nicklaus does, in terms of spinning the ball and stopping it. They fall somewhere in between Jack Nicklaus and the average male golfer in that regard. You will see some LPGA players hitting bump-and-run shots, or high soft lobs that land fairly dead because they don't all spin the ball like a male golfer.

Troubleshooting: Positive Thoughts, Positive Results

Watch closely when the pros get into trouble—and watch how they respond. What happens is that a shot out of trouble is so difficult or so tricky that the player focuses totally on what he or she is doing. Their concentration is heightened. They might play a recovery shot better than they would an 8-iron from the middle of the fairway, because they don't let anything distract them—because the price they are going to pay if they don't pull this off is too great.

What too often happens when you get into trouble is that rather than concentrating on what it takes to execute the shot to get you out of the trouble, your mind wanders *to the trouble* and to the things that might go wrong. That invariably leads to the very thing you are trying to avoid. Have positive thoughts and focus on where you want to go.

If I have to weave the ball through two trees and keep it kind of low and hit a hard runner, I work so hard on getting that thing aimed right and hitting the ball with a square clubface to knock it right through that hole in the trees that I don't think about hitting a tree on the right or on the left. If I did, I would hit it. I can assure you that pros are not thinking about what could go wrong. They are thinking about how to do this right.

I once played a shot at Mission Hills in the Dinah Shore tournament, back in the 1970s. It was the par-5 18th hole and there was water up by the left side about 170 or 180 yards short of the green. I had hit my second shot pretty hard left and short. I had trees and a bush in front of me and there was seemingly no way I could play to the green. The pin was on the far left side of the green. As I explained to my caddie what I was going to do, you could hear him breathing. I finally gripped way down on my 5-wood and I started the ball out over the middle of the water, almost at a condo, and hit this big slice back on the green. I pulled the shot off perfectly and made a birdie.

Two things happened there. I was completely focused on what I wanted to do, and I mechanically executed the shot well. One complements the other. If you don't believe you can do something, you might be better off not to try it. You probably won't hit the shot well. You should chip out, instead.

I do believe people have become too precise and analytical about their games as a result of watching golf on television. You see the pros lining up their putts from all angles and think you have to do the same. You don't. On television, everything is analyzed, dissected, and computed. If you watch a man or woman professional on TV in a big tournament, they know within two yards how far they are going to hit a 5-iron. They do—and you don't. So enjoy *your* life in golf and play a little bit more naturally. Have fun!

14

THE MENTAL SIDE

Smart Strategy and Staying Positive

Most golf courses aren't designed for women, and that creates special problems. A 6,000-yard golf course is too long for the average woman, and making a score of "par" on many—indeed the majority of—holes is unrealistic for many women, especially beginners. Some progress has been made in the design and creation of more forward tees that reduce the length of a regulation course and allow women to enjoy the game, but more needs to be done. It's not much fun loving a game but realizing basically (to quote my colleague Bob Rosburg) that you've got "no chance" on most of the holes you play to ever reach the green in regulation numbers.

Perhaps what needs to be done is to adjust the concept of par. Take a typical par 4 of 390 yards (see diagram). If you are able to hit the ball 150 yards, off the tee, then obviously you are not going to be able to get to the green until your third shot. You've simply got to concentrate on putting your drive in the fairway—always the first, most crucial step—and then advancing your second shot another 140 to 150 yards and put yourself in position to get on the green in three. You've got to plot your second shot so you're left with a distance you're most comfortable with for your third shot. For example, if you are better hitting a full 7- or 8-iron from 100 yards, hit a second shot that will leave you as close to that distance as possible. If you happen to get your third shot close and make a 4, it's really like a birdie for you.

The realistic par for most women golfers on a hole of over 300 yards is 5. Because of the length of golf courses, women golfers can really use a good short game. Being a good wedge player and a good fairway wood player are probably the two ways that most women can improve—in addition to gaining distance.

Longer holes can really be killers. The 490- or 500-yard par 5 is at least a par 6 for women. Again, you've got to be a good plotter and planner and avoid costly mistakes that run up your score. The trouble that does not come

PAR 4, 390 YARDS: PLOT YOUR WAY TO THE EASIEST APPROACH SHOT. *On a par-4 hole approaching 400 yards, most women can't get to the green with two good shots. You have to accept your distance capabilities and plan so that you give yourself the easiest possible third shot into the green—and a chance to maybe "steal" a par.*

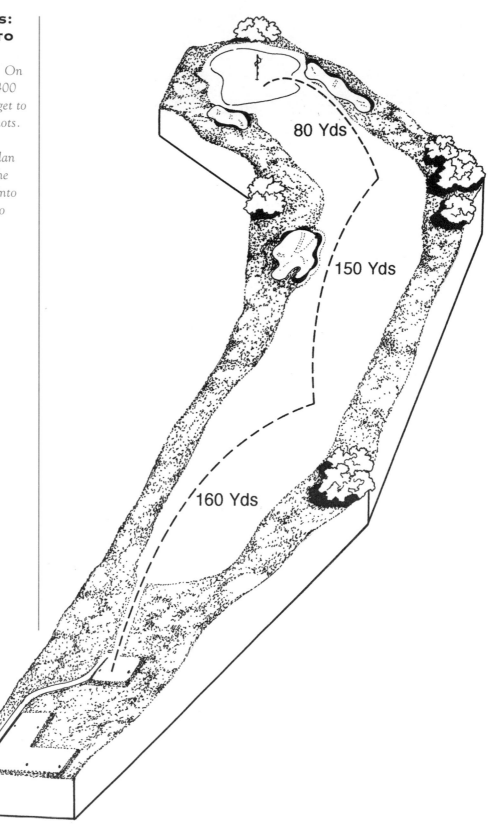

80 Yds

150 Yds

160 Yds

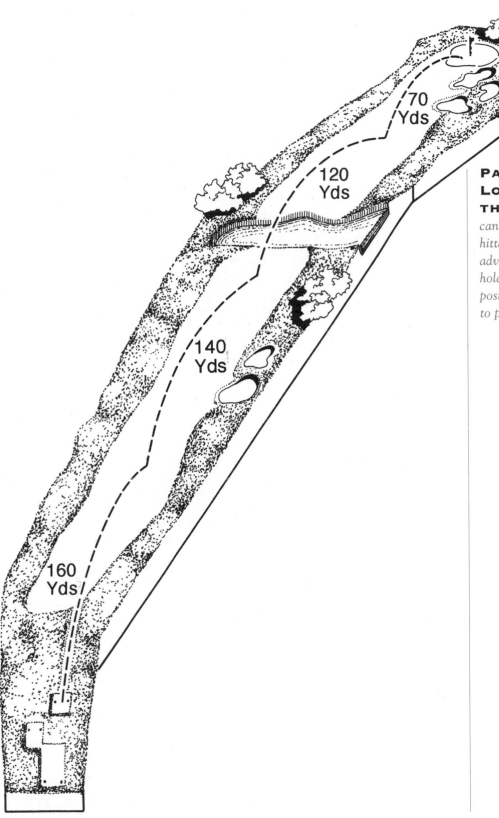

70
Yds

120
Yds

140
Yds

160
Yds

**PAR 5, 490 YARDS:
LONG HOLES TAKE
THEIR TOLL.** *Par-5 holes
can be killers if you're a short
hitter. Concentrate on
advancing the ball toward the
hole in increments—focus
positively on where you want
to place each shot.*

JACK NICKLAUS

Winner of 20 major championships

"Many golfers of both sexes try to play beyond their capabilities, but I think higher-handicap women in particular hurt themselves that way. For instance, if your strength isn't sufficient to get home in two shots on a tough par 4, don't risk your entire round by trying. Hit the green comfortably in three and be sure of a bogey if you don't one-putt.

"Remember, the scoring at golf is as much about avoiding disasters as making birdies. Be realistic and be patient."

into play for many men, or from which they can escape more easily—especially from rough—wreaks havoc with women. Hazards or rough areas that men drive right over can be in play for women. Sometimes, you just have to shoot away from that trouble, or lay up short and not take an unnecessary risk.

However, this isn't much fun, and when you have a chance to be aggressive and pull off a shot, I think you should go for it as often as not. That's the joy of golf—encountering a difficult situation and responding to the challenge. The best players make good decisions, and once made, they concentrate on execution.

Play your natural shot as often as possible, be it a draw or a fade. When you are faced with a hole that demands a shot contrary to what you're comfortable with, you will still be better off hitting your natural shot—even if it means starting the ball at the edge of a hazard and curving it back onto safe ground. Trying to force a shot you are not comfortable with does not work, nine times out of ten.

Today's golf information highway is so packed with advice on every kind of situation that many people are trying to play the game too analytically. The end result is a lack of touch and feel and any natural motion to fall back on. Beware of this "paralysis by analysis."

Imagery

In all situations, particularly tough ones, imagining the flight of your ball and where you would like it to land—almost visualizing it to the spot where you want it to finish—can be an effective tool. If you can't form a mental picture of a shot you're trying to play, odds are you won't be able to play the shot. I actually picture the flight of my ball as I stand behind it, before I've even taken my address position. If you haven't already, you will experience standing behind a putt and knowing you're going to make it. It's an unexplainable phenomenon, and is the most classic example of positive imagery.

Confidence

Maintaining a positive mental attitude stems from a feeling of assurance when standing over a golf shot. Confidence builds with good shots and success. We are all capable of concentrating on one shot—and one hole—at a time. When you are systematically trying to lower your scores you must in fact do this. The enormity of breaking 100, 90, or 80 for the first time will overwhelm you if you think about it on the first tee. Take care of each hole, which is all you are capable of, and the total score will take care of itself.

For golfers, our brains seem to shrink as we near the course. I've often thought that Lucy from "Peanuts" could get rich if she'd place her psychiatrist booth 20 yards from the first tee. It is amazing how people sometimes change from the practice tee to the first tee, both mentally and emotionally. Their muscles tighten and their thought process gets all bound up, too.

Patience is definitely a virtue in this game. Don't get too excited when you start to play well, trying to lower your score all of a sudden. Or when you do have a bad hole, don't try to recoup it all at once. If you try to eagle or birdie the next hole, you'll only compound your problems. Confidence and patience are intertwined. If you're confident, you can recover from a bad spell; you'll be patient enough not to try to get it all back with one swing. You simply cannot do that, although we've all tried. Concentrate on the present, forget the past, and don't look too far ahead.

Adapting to Conditions

Much of golf is adjusting and adapting. I remember when I first went to Scotland as a 16-year-old for the British Amateur at Carnoustie. My father and I were very rigid in our thinking that I could play with the game I had. I tried to fly shots into greens that were rock-hard. I also tried to just take more club into the wind instead of learning how to hit a good "knock-down" shot. I was not very successful. I did not adapt. I lost in the first round to a girl who had not been playing golf very long. And I was ready to give up the game because I was so frustrated.

Years later, I went back to the European Open at Sunningdale in England and had a lot of success. It became my favorite tournament. A lot of it had to do with a caddie I hooked up with. He was a local legend who had caddied there for 50 years named Ron Mullins; I just called him Mullins, and he called me Madam. He had all this local knowledge of the course at Sunningdale and he would imbue me with it, steering me around and telling me exactly what kind of shots to play under the circumstances. I had confidence in him; I listened and I adapted, and became a more versatile player as a result.

Professional golf is played in so many varied conditions. The same is true for you. You adapt going to high altitudes where you gain yardage in the light air. You immediately jump into that situation. But most adjustments are

BETH DANIEL

31-time LPGA winner and three-time Player of the Year

"Women golfers have to play smarter, because golf courses aren't really designed for us. So you need better course management. Your golf pro or somebody can help you navigate your way around the course. If you know you're going to have a hard time carrying a bunker, then play for the opening and try to two-putt. Even off the tee, you need to plan, so that after you drive you'll have an easier fairway wood or iron shot into that opening on your next shot. You need to plan, plan ahead and stick to that plan."

a little more difficult. Here are some of the things you might encounter that will require you to adjust:

- If you suddenly find yourself playing a course where the turf is very firm and there's not a lot of cushiony grass underneath the ball, that's a time to run pitches into greens rather than trying to throw the ball up in the air.

- If you find a course with very hard greens, don't fight what nature presents. Adapt. Take what the course gives you. Land the ball shorter than you normally would and allow it to roll up to the flagstick.

- If you find greens that are exceptionally slow, firm up your grip to hit your putts with a little more authority. If you play early in the morning and the greens are wet, it will also require you to hit your putts harder than you normally would.

- A very wet golf course. Consider hitting a 3-wood from the tee, because your drives are not going to run very far at all. You'll need to carry the ball and you'll need to carry the ball as far as possible.

- Rain and wet conditions. Do what you can to keep your equipment dry. Try to "pick" the ball a little more from the turf, making as little contact with the ground as possible. Gripping down on the club slightly will aid you in this effort.

- In playing from the forward or women's tees, be aware that very often, they are set on the *right* side of the fairway. This is not a particularly appealing place to drive from all the time. It's difficult to align correctly from the far right of the fairway back to the center. But it's important to maintaining a good golf swing that you check your alignment from time to time. If you don't align well in this situation, you're in jeopardy of pulling the ball or being a slicer.

- Windy conditions. We've covered this separately in Chapter 9. But you are adapting when you make the necessary club and adjustments and technique changes.

Remember, conditions change daily, even if you're playing the same course. How you adapt will have a lot to do with your ability to score.

Ultimately, you have to learn to accept what happens to you in all conditions and situations. I remember playing in the first tournament of the 1976 LPGA season at Kendall Lakes in Miami. I started on the tenth hole, a par 5. I had a 7-iron for my third shot and hit what looked like a real good shot.

HELEN ALFREDSSON

1993 Nabisco Dinah Shore champion

"If you're trying to lower your handicap, you have to play to your abilities. Don't try to hit it over the water when you can't possibly clear the water. It's ridiculous. Hit it up there short and then play the next shot. Little things like that can add up. Why try to go for the pin when it's an impossible shot? So be smart, and know when to play a safe shot."

Unfortunately, it landed in a bunker and buried so deep that there was a question of whether I could get it out. I took the hardest swing I could; the ball went straight into the air and came back down and hit my club. That's a penalty, and I made an 8 on that hole. I went on to win the tournament and have the best year of my professional life. So there is something to be said for not giving up and letting a bad hole ruin your round. Remember, adversity can either make you better or make you worse.

In conclusion, I urge you not to confuse playing smart with playing scared. At times, taking chances is part of progress.

15

GIVING AND TAKING LESSONS

Building Rapport and Creating Independence

My father was my primary teacher. Ours was a trial-and-error method of learning. I also was privileged to receive lessons from some very special people along the way, especially Bob Green and Bob Toski. After leaving the tour, I have devoted some of my own time to giving lessons back home in Texas and recently took part in a couple of Jack Nicklaus–Jim Flick Golf Schools. It is an interesting experience. Usually I try to have students hit a few balls without my saying much. It takes them a while to get comfortable, because they know they are being observed. Often, they will tell you what they think they're doing wrong. Students must be good listeners and the teacher a good communicator, and you must be on the same wavelength.

I tell the students to hit some balls and try to forget that I'm there. "Do it the way you normally do and just let me watch," I say. I try to talk to them a minute or two beforehand and find out, when they hit the ball poorly, if there is a pattern to their mistakes. Is there one bad shot they hit more often than others? And then I might watch them while they hit 8 to 10 balls. Sometimes after the first two balls you spot something that they should change. You don't want to simply focus on changing right away, but instead offer gentle, positive reinforcement. You have to establish a rapport and a comfort level.

Even the best players are constantly working on their games. I'm sure you've read and heard about the famous "gurus" who oversee the games of Nick Faldo, Nick Price, Greg Norman, Betsy King, Jan Stephenson, etc. If they're taking lessons after all these years, then it's a good bet most other golfers will need lessons, at least occasionally. It's really the simplest, best way to get better—even better than reading a book like this, I must admit—provided you have a thoughtful teacher.

The best teachers quickly separate, in an individual, what is a bad habit and what is an idiosyncrasy—that is, a habit that may be unorthodox but that works for them after years and years of playing.

A Fundamental Approach

I'd be inclined to look for a teacher who stresses more fundamentals—the tried-and-true things that we know work because they've been proved over

THE GIVE-AND-TAKE OF TEACHING. *Here I am with a favorite (although somewhat stubborn) pupil—my husband, Yippy. Learning the game from a spouse can be fraught with peril. You're best off getting an introductory lesson from a trained professional.*

time. Beware of someone who has the new-and-different, faddish kind of idea or theory. Not that you might not get something out of it, but a lot of those theories are exactly that, a theory—and in practice, they don't always work. Someone once told me, "Beware of someone with a theory." I certainly think that's good advice relative to golf instruction. Certain principles are correct and work for a great number of people. But beware of the teacher who thinks there's only one way to play for every person, because we know better than that, just from watching those who have been successful in golf and the many different styles they employ. Just like the grip I'm teaching you: I concede not everyone subscribes to it, and that's fine. That's what makes horse-racing (and golf instruction) so interesting.

When you're looking for a teacher, you don't want to go to somebody who says this is going to be an eight-month overhaul and you're going to have to hit 4.2 million balls. That might make some sense for a tour pro, but not for someone who's playing golf mainly for the fun of it. You don't want to meet this guy . . . or gal. You want somebody who's going to say, "Well, you have some good beginnings here, and I see some things that we can build on, and maybe change a couple of things. Just a few fundamental changes, and you can be a better player than you are." If you are a serious player trying to take your game to a higher competitive level, you might want a more in-depth program. But those individuals are few and far between.

Before taking a lesson, it's important for you to try to clear you mind of your old habits. It's human nature to resist. And there's a lot of information that golfers have misapplied or overdone. So at least for these 30 minutes or an hour, try to do whatever the teacher is asking you to do. There just might be a revelation there. If you're not open to something new, then you probably shouldn't be taking a lesson. If you discover after the fact that some of it doesn't work for you, then you can discard it, but at least give yourself a chance to try it and understand it.

The most common error I see when I give lessons is in address position and posture. Only physical limitations should keep you from a good setup. Most people I see tend to have the ball too far back in their stance and they aim too far to the right. That gets them started to being an over-the-top type of swinger, because subconsciously they know they are aimed to the right and they're trying to get the ball started back on their target line. These are fairly basic, fundamental things that can be easily fixed if the student is willing to make the necessary changes.

The longer you go without good instruction, the more deeply ingrained bad habits become—another good reason for starting golf and getting good instruction early on.

Golf schools are an excellent "crash course" in learning. They provide concentrated instruction with practice, drills, and someone to monitor your changes and improvements closely. Students at the schools tend to be highly motivated, and they can get better fairly quickly. However, the downside is that these schools are quite expensive, and thus unaffordable to many. Also, spending time with the same instructors is at best a year or two away.

Helping Yourself

The ideal of any teacher-student relationship is to create independence, so that students can eventually help themselves.

First—and do this whenever your game slips—go back to the basics, checking elementary things such as ball position, alignment, etc. The pros do this as a matter of course.

It's important to read what your ball does, more by the path it starts on and less by the curves near the end of its flight. If the ball starts left of your target, that is sure proof that the path of your swing is coming across the intended swing path to the target. If the ball starts to the right, it's more than likely you are unable to let the club release through impact. Sometimes, undue tension and tightness in your arms and hands is the culprit here.

Restoring Your Golf (and Your Self-) Esteem

It's human nature to revert to your bad habits and the things that hurt you. When you are really at a loss for understanding what you are doing wrong, you have to go back to the drawing board. Go to the practice tee, take a 7-iron and put a row of balls on a tee, and just start swinging freely, without much thought. Hit little three-quarter, free-muscle kinds of swings, until you can start popping the ball solidly off the tee again. This will renew your confidence and restore your faith that this game is not as difficult as you've been making it.

When your confidence is renewed and you can swing freely and rhythmically again, hitting the ball flush, then try to impart those feelings to your normal golf swing again.

Remember, the 7-iron is the club I recommend that beginners start with. And when things get bad, you should go back to it. I think the 7-iron is a confidence builder. It's a club that, if you're doing anything right, will work.

I like to equate this recovery to when you're in the hospital and in pain. The doctor will say, "Tell us when you first start to have pain, because we can control it. If you let it get too bad, then it's difficult for us to control." The same thing happens with your golf swing. Your slump deepens and deepens and sud-

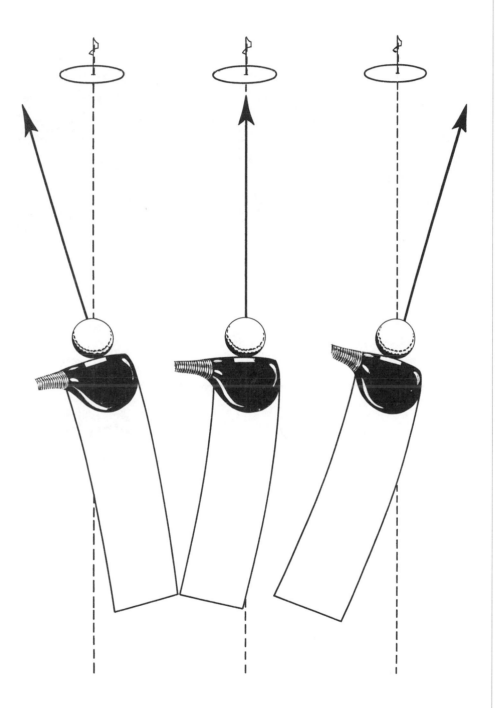

READING YOUR BALL. *The path the ball starts on will teach you a lot about how you've swung. If the ball starts to the right, you haven't allowed the clubface to release through impact (right). If you've kept the club on the target line and the clubface is square, the ball will start straight (middle). If the ball starts to the left of your target, your swing has come across your intended path (left).*

denly you haven't played decently for six months. Not only are your mechanical problems more ingrained, but your confidence is low—a big hole to climb out of. You don't want to let that happen. A lot of the game is about building confidence in your ability and believing that you can perform.

THE RECOVERY DRILL. *When things start going badly, I recommend going back to the 7-iron and hitting a row of teed-up balls "machine-gun" style. Just swinging* *freely and concentrating on making solid contact is a great way to clear your mind of negative thoughts and renew your confidence.*

16
KEEPING IT FUN

I lost my mother to illness as a young child, and through golf my father and I spent a great deal of time together. He was a demanding teacher, but his perseverance and caring made me better and better. Certainly golf has made my life much better and out of the ordinary.

I remember so many of the wonderful experiences that I've had because of golf—the people I've met and the places I've seen. I still remember meeting JoAnne Carner when I was 11 years old and she was 17. She had won the National Junior Girls' Championship in Toledo, Ohio. She was a phenom herself back then, even as an amateur player. She was JoAnne Gunderson, "The Great Gundy." You can imagine how I looked up to her, and I can still recall how nice she was to me and my dad. When she joined the tour, we remained friends and won the National Team Championship in 1977. It was a bit of a struggle, I admit. Our personalities and style of golf were quite dissimilar. I was such an intense player, and JoAnne would break out laughing when she did something horrid. It was probably good for me to play with someone who could laugh at herself like that. We all need to lighten up. That's why JoAnne has endured so long—because she takes such joy in playing and has never lost her sense of humor.

Golf is a game more full of variables than most. It's never the same, and you're always learning. The golf course changes, you change, the weather changes, your playing partners change, your goals change—but the challenge remains the same. It's you against the course—and that little white ball. Golf can become an addiction and an obsession. You have to guard against loving the game so much that you hate it. It's wise to avoid extreme emotions. If it were an easy game, everyone would be playing it well. Obviously, if you go out to any golf course in this country, you'll see that this is not the case. But good fundamentals—and the right attitude and approach—can go a long way toward making your golf experience all the more enjoyable. The key thing is to not lose sight of the fact that this is a *game*.

The game is more accessible now to everyone. All the tours—LPGA, PGA, and Senior PGA—have great programs to introduce the game to juniors and, in many cases, make equipment available. Junior clinics and com-

IN THE WINNER'S CIRCLE. *With Dinah Shore in 1976, after one of the biggest wins of my career.*

petitions can be found across the country. So the future would seem to be bright. If you are just getting started, you've made a great choice.

Is there more than one effective way to play the game? Certainly. What's detailed in these pages, though, made for my success and that of other players I've seen. The game is addictive because none of us ever totally masters it—but there are moments of great success that keep us all coming back for more. I think you will enjoy some success if you put these ideas into practice.

THE RANKIN FILE

Judy Torluemke Rankin
Born: February 18, 1945, St. Louis, Missouri.
Height: 5'4.
Weight: 120.
Family: Husband, Walter (Yippy); son, Tuey.
Home: Midland, Texas.

Career Highlights

AMATEUR
- Four-time National Pee Wee Champion, 1953-1956.
- Won 1959 Missouri Amateur at age 14, the youngest ever to take the state title, and won again in 1961.
- Low amateur in 1960 U.S. Women's Open at Worchester (Massachusetts) Country Club.

PROFESSIONAL
- Joined LPGA Tour in 1962 as 17-year-old.
- First victory: 1968 Corpus Christi Open.
- Between 1968 and 1979, accumulated 27 victories, including the 1976 Colgate Dinah Shore Winner's Circle and the 1977 Peter Jackson Classic, both now designated "majors" on the LPGA Tour.
- Two-time leading money winner and LPGA Player of the Year (1976 and 1977).
- In 1976, won six tournaments and set a new single-season earnings record of $150,734, becoming the first LPGA player in history to cross $100,000 threshold in a season.
- Winner of three Vare Trophies for low stroke average on LPGA Tour: 1973 (73.08), 1976 (72.25), and 1977 (72.16).
- Set a record (which still stands) in 1977 for most top-10 finishes in one season with 25.
- Two-time European Open champion (1974 and 1977).
- Last victory: 1979 WUI Classic.
- Due to chronic back problems, played the tour sporadically in the early 1980s and underwent back surgery in 1985.

- Inducted into the Texas Golf Hall of Fame in 1987 and into the All-American Collegiate Hall of Fame in 1993.
- Named nonplaying captain of 1996 LPGA Tour Solheim Cup team for matches against Europe in Chepstow, Wales.

TELEVISION

- Was guest analyst for CBS on Mixed Team Championship in 1978.
- Joined ABC Sports as on-course commentator in 1984.
- Is only female commentator who is a regular on both men's and women's events.
- Has covered three of the men's majors: the U.S. and British Open and PGA Championship, for ABC.
- Serves as ABC's main analyst for LPGA events.

INDEX

Acceleration, 62
Address, 37, 183
Adversity, coping with, xiv
Aiming to right of target, 33
Air time, 97
Alfredsson, Helen, 43–44, 62, 160, 168, 178
Alignment, 29–35
  aids on putters, 157
Alliss, Peter, 40
Anxiety attack, 80
Approaching top of swing, 44–46
Arm stretch, 140
Azinger, Paul, 11, 69, 131

Backswing, 37, 128
  of putt, 79
Bad habits, 183, 184
Bad lies, 132
Balance, 9, 23
Ball, lie of, 107
Ball position, 26–29
  for pitch shot, 97, 99–100
Beginnings
  basics, 9–10
  grip, 5–7
  short swing, 7–9
Bending your knees, 26
Bent Tree Golf and Country Club (Sarasota), vii
Berg, Patty, 161
Bermuda grass, 90
Best-ball, 3
Blister, 9
Block, 137
Bounce of club, 109
Bowen, Nanci, 157
Bradley, Pat, 38, 165
British Amateur, 177
Bump-and-run, 105
Bunker play, 109–125
  buried lies, 117–120
  chipping in, 120–122
  on fairway, 122–123
  setup, 110–116
  slopes and angles, 116–117
Buried lies, in bunker play, 117–120
Burton, Brandie, 159

Caddie grip, 11
Calcavecchia, Mark, 61, 168
Caponi, Donna, 11
Carner, JoAnne, 115, 131, 164, 187
Center-shafted putters, 155
Centrifugal force, 49
Children
  early exposure to golf, 4
  learning golf, xi
Chipping, 2, 93–97
  in bunker play, 120–122
  club selection for, 96–97
Clearing left side, 47
Closed stance, 35
Clubface
  angle of, 51
  opening, 109
  and setting feet, 31
Clubhead, weight of, 150
Clubs
  alignment of, 31
  bounce of, 109
Clubs, See also Equipment
  selecting for chipping, 96–97
  selecting for wind, 128
College programs, 160
Combination stroke, 75, 96
Coming over top, 49
Competition, 3
  women in, 162
Compression, 158
Confidence, 176–177, 184
Couples, Fred, 11, 45, 69
Crenshaw, Ben, 84
Cross-handed putting method, 69
Curtis Cup, 3

Daly, John, 11, 61
Daniel, Beth, 62, 69, 164–165, 177
Davies, Laura, 45, 66, 164
Dead hands, 74–75, 85
Distance, 62–68
  inability to generate, xii
Divots, 50, 52
Downhill lie, 133
  in bunkers, 116–117
Downhill putt, 87–88
Draw, 35
Drivers, 5, 150–152

8-iron, 104, 105, 107, 120
Els, Ernie, 61
Equipment, 147–158
  drivers, 150–152
  gloves, 158
  grip size, 148–149
  putters, 155–157
  set composition, 148
  shafts, 149
  utility woods, 154–155
  weight and speed, 150
European Open, 177
Exercise, 139–146
Explosion shot, 109
Eyes on ball, 80

Fade, 35
"Fairway Bird," x
Fairway bunkers, 122–123
Faldo, Nick, 69
Fast greens, 85
Fitness trailer, 145
5-iron, 133
Flat area, 79, 80
Flexing your knees, 26
Floyd, Raymond, 168
Forward tees, 178
4-iron, 133
Full swing, 37–68
  approaching top, 44–46
  head movement, 49–50
  motion in, 37
  swing plane, 46–47
  tempo and timing, 61
  trigger at top, 47–49
  weight shift, 42–44
  wrist cock, 38

Gloves, 158
Goetze, Vicki, 168
Golf balls, 157–158
Golf course
  first time on, 2
  length of, 173
Golf Digest, ix
Grain of grass, reading, 90–91
Graphite, 149
Grass, 104–105
Green, Bob, 1, 147

Green
    adjusting to, 178
    reading, 87
    reading grain, 90–91
    speed and club choices for
        chipping, 97
Grip, 5–7, 11–22
    for putting, 69–71
    right-hand, 17, 19
Grip pressure, 9
Grip size, 148–149
Ground time, 97

Hagge, Marlene, 11, 63, 161
Hamstring stretches, 142
Hand strength, 146
Handicap, 3
Head movement, 49–50
Health clubs, 140
Heel-shafted putters, 155
High shot, 135
Higuchi, Chako, 50
Hip restriction, on backswing,
    43
Hitting balls, to gain strength,
    139
Hitting practice balls, 2
Hooding clubface, 99
Hook, 12, 35, 135–136

Imagery, 176
Injury, avoiding, 145
Inkster, Juli, 3, 67, 91
Interlocking grip, 21
Irons, 132, 148, 152–153
Irwin, Hale, 67

Jacobsen, Peter, 80
JC Penney Classic (Florida), ix
Jones, Bobby, 45
Junior clinics, 4

Kendall Lakes (Miami), 178–179
Kick point, 149
King, Betsy, 47, 165–166
Kite, Tom, 37, 63, 69, 79

Langer, Bernhard, 11
Leadbetter, David, 44
Left-hand grip, 19
    benefits of strong, 12–13, 14
Legs, role in golf swing, 64
Lessons, 2, 181–186
    fundamental approach in,
        182–184
    helping yourself, 184
    learning from television, 180

Lie of ball, 107
    bad, 132
    unusual, 133
Lies of irons, 152–153
Little, Sally, 44, 84
Littler, Gene, 163
Lob shot, 100–104
Loft, 104
Lopez, Nancy, x, 11, 37, 45, 61,
    75, 79, 85, 163–164
Love, Davis Jr., ix
Love, Davis III, 64
Low shot, 133–135
LPGA tour, 4, 159–166
    comparisons, 160–161
    scholarships and support, 160

Male golfers, xiv
Melnyk, Steve, 9, 65
Mental side of golf, xiv, 173–179
    adapting to conditions,
        177–179
    confidence, 176–177
    imagery, 176
Miniature golf, 10
Mission Hills, 171
Modified tray position, 38, 40
Motion, 37
"Moving off the ball," 50
Mowry, Larry, 117
Musberger, Brent, 169
Muscles, big and small, 44

National Golf Foundation, xi
Natural shot, 176
Neutral grip, 15
Nicklaus, Jack, 12, 37, 84,
    131–132, 176
9-iron, 120
Norman, Greg, 111, 145, 168

One-handed swing, 38, 41
One-piece takeaway, 37–38
Open stance, 35
Opening clubface, 109
Orthodox grip, 12, 15
Overlapping grip, 21
Overlocking grip, 21

Palmer, Sandra, 115, 161
Par, 173
Par for women, xiii
Paralysis by analysis, 176
Patience, 177
Penick, Harvey, 86–87
Pepper, Dottie, 68, 80
PGA tour, 4

Pistol grip, 18, 22
Pitching, 97–107
Pitching wedge, 100, 148
Player, Gary, 75
Playing matches, 3
Plumb-bobbing, 88
Positive thoughts, 170–171
Post, Sandra, 64
Posture, 9, 23–26, 67, 183
    for putting, 82, 84
Power, 63
Practice balls, hitting, 2
Practice putting green, 2
"Pro Talker," x
Pull hook, 135
Putters, 9, 155–157
    alignment aids on, 157
    sweet spot of, 87
Putting, 69–92
    backswing in, 79
    downhill, 87–88
    from off the green, 91
    posture for, 82, 84
    reading grain, 90–91
    routine in, 84
    setup, 72–74
    speed for, 88, 90, 91–92
    stroke for, 74–84
Putting green, 86

Quiet hands, 180

Rain, 178
Range ball, 86
Rankin grip, 12
Regulation courses, xiii
Release, 51
Repetition, 61
Reverse overlap grip, 69
Reverse pivot, 44, 49, 64
Right-hand grip, 17
Risk taking, 168–169
Robbins, Kelly, 11, 47
Rosburg, Bob, 49, 150
Rough, 131–132
Routine, in putting, 84
Runner's stretch, 142
Ryder Cup, 3

Sand See bunker play
Sand wedge, 100, 104, 107,
    109–110, 148, 153–154
Scramble format, 3
Set position, 127–128
Setup, 183
    for bunker play, 110–116
    for chipping, 93

for putting, 72–74
  for unusual lie, 133
7-iron, 5, 104, 105, 107, 184
"7-iron, 30-day" trial period, 5
Shafts, 149
Sheehan, Patty, 161, 165, 168, 180
Short swing, 7–9
Shoulders, 35
  stretching, 140
6-iron, 105, 107
Slice, 12, 33, 50, 137
Solheim Cup, 3
Specialized shots, 127–137
  to punch out of trees, 133–135
Speed, 51, 65
  equipment weight and, 150
  in long putt, 88, 90
  for putting, 72, 91–92
Spin on shot, 35
Splash shot, 111
Spot alignment, 32
Spot technique, for bunker play,
    116
Square stance, 35
Stacy, Hollis, 44, 112, 116
Stance
  ball position and, 27–28
  for chipping, 93
  width of, 31, 35
Steel shafts, 149
Stephenson, Jan, 66, 69, 149, 168
Stewart, Payne, 157
Stockton, Dave, 84
Stockton, Dave, Jr., 26
Strange, Curtis, 49, 67, 104, 115
Strength, 5
  in hands, 146
  hitting balls to gain, 139

Stretching, 139–146
Stroke, 9–10
  length and putting distance, 77
  for putting, 74–84
Strong grip, vii, 11, 41, 51
Suggs, Louise, 65, 161
Sweeper, 26
Sweet spot, of putter, 87
Swing, See also full swing
  leaving, 1
  for low shot, 133–135
  one-handed, 38, 41
  role of legs in, 64
  short, 7–9
Swing path, 51
Swing plane, 46–47
Swing weight, 150

Takeaway, 38, 39
Target line, 29
Tee shots, 151
Teeing ball, 52
Tees, 7
  forward, 178
Television, 167–171
  criticism and feedback, 167–168
  learning by watching, 180
Tempo, 61, 116
Ten-finger grip, 21
Texas wedge, 97
Texas wedge shot, 91
3-iron, 133
3-wood, 31
Timing, 38, 61
Top of swing, approaching, 44–46
Toski, Bob, 2, 180
Tournament for beginners, 2–3
Trees, punching out of, 133–135

Trevino, Lee, 61
Turf, adjusting to, 178
Two-piece balls, 157

Uphill lie, 133
  in bunkers, 116–117
U.S. Women's Open, 11, 168
Utility woods, 154–155

"V" test, 15–16
Vardon grip, 21

Waggle, 37
Walker Cup, 3
Walking, 145–146
Weak grip, 11
Wedge shot
  alignment for, 31
  Texas, 91, 97
Wedges, 5, 97, 148
Weight of equipment, 150
Weight shift, 42–44
Wet golf course, 178
Whitworth, Kathy, 159, 163
Width of stance, 35
Wilson, Helen Sigel, xi
Wind, 31, 127–131, 178
  hitting into, 128–131
Women's tees, 178
Woods, 132
  utility, 154–155
Wound balls, 157
Wright, Mickey, 159, 163
Wrists, 8
  in bunker play, 117
  cock in full swing, 38

Yips, 80